# The Littlest Bell Ringer

By
Carol Grace Stratton

Illustrated by
Ruth Korch

# *Dedication*

This book is dedicated to Juniper Sage Brown, who is terribly missed and is probably ringing bells in heaven.

# Acknowledgements

Thank you to Rowena for her thorough editing and for my beta readers, who helped me see any holes in the story. And as for my wonderful illustrator, Ruth, thank you for being able to imagine my story. Your illustrations brought this story to life. Marion Ward Durham, I am grateful for your insights into the Red Kettle campaign and the Salvation Army. And finally, thanks to God who is the original author of life and all of its stories.

# Table of Contents

1. Dad's Hurt! ............................................... 1
2. New Netherlands ..................................... 9
3. Ugly Shoes ............................................. 17
4. Who Tripped Me? .................................. 27
5. Class Projects ........................................ 33
6. Stomach Ache ........................................ 41
7. Scrabble................................................. 47
8. Story of the Red Kettle........................... 55
9. Letter to Poppi ...................................... 63
10. Help!.................................................... 69
11. Mom's Home!....................................... 75
12. It's Official........................................... 81
13. Best Friends.......................................... 89
14. Trouble................................................ 93
15. Class Spy ............................................. 99
16. No Singing.......................................... 103
17. Field Trip ........................................... 109
18. Emergency.......................................... 115
19. Counting Money .................................. 121
20. Life's Not Fair ..................................... 125
21. Burglars.............................................. 135
22. Mom Heads to School .......................... 141
23. Bell Ringing is Hard............................. 147
24. Dare to Sing........................................ 151

25. The Snitch............................................................. 157
26. Mom's Story.......................................................... 163
27. A Golden Moment ............................................. 169

# —Chapter One—

## *Dad's Hurt*

"No, Lord, no."

My mother let out a piercing scream as if Jesus had come back for the Rapture and forgotten her. I watched as she dropped her cell phone onto the tile floor in the kitchen. The glass cover shattered into a million pieces, creating an ugly webbed crystal.

I picked the phone up and placed it on the counter. Then I followed my mother into the living room, where she huddled in the corner of our blue sofa, rolled up into a ball like a potato bug. Now that was scary.

"Mom!" I put my hands on her shoulders and shook her. "What happened?"

She looked up, her round eyes an empty stare. My hands grew cold, and I trembled all over.

"What?" I waited for an answer, but all she did was rock back and forth like she was putting a small baby to sleep, which seemed strange as I was her only child. "Sh-sh-should I call Miss Katie?"

She nodded, the tiniest movement.

I picked up the receiver of the old landline in the kitchen and dialed our neighbor who lived three doors down. "Miss Katie, come quickly, something's wrong with Mom." I put the phone down and sat beside my mother, my head spinning. She had been so calm all these months my dad had been gone overseas. It must be something to do with him. "Is it Poppi? Is he … is he dead?"

My mother shook her head and burst into a wail. I felt helpless and hoped Miss Katie would come soon. Maybe she could talk to her.

It seemed like an eternity, but finally I heard a knock on the door. I raced and threw the door open. "She won't tell me what happened." The tears I had held back now streamed over my face. I hadn't been this scared for all of my ten years. Miss Katie, a round jolly lady, flew through the front door and patted me on the hand.

"He's been hurt, Kate." My mother blurted out the words as she rocked back and forth.

Miss Katie lowered her body onto the sofa next to Mom. "Tell me what happened."

Mom went on to explain she had had a call from the Army. The officer said my dad, who had been stationed in Kabul, Afghanistan, had been clearing out a room in a vacant apartment building. Things had looked good until he crossed the room to examine a pile of rubble. "Back off," he told his men. He took one step closer to the pile and stepped on an IED, an unexploded bomb, and it blew up.

"He's lucky to be alive but ..." Mom gripped the sofa's arm, kneading it with her hands. "Kate, he's lost both legs."

All I remembered was the room spinning as I hit the carpet. The next thing I knew, I was in my bed, the back of my head throbbing and Miss Katie and Mom each holding up one finger, asking me how many fingers I saw. I figured my mom was worried about me because she puckers her lips when upset, and right now she looked like she was ready to whistle as she hovered over me with a glass of orange juice.

I shook my head, "No," and closed my eyes, wanting to will away that awful phone call. They left the room, but I heard Miss Katie and Mom speak in hushed tones in the family room and learned more of the terrible details. He was now at Walter Reed Hospital on the East Coast and would be there for a long time. They would be able to reconstruct his nose and repair the skin burnt off of his right arm, but his legs were gone. "He will be fitted with prosthetic legs, and it will take months rehab for him to be able to walk."

I didn't know what rehab was, but it didn't sound good. I cried myself to sleep that night, knowing my daddy would never be able to pick me up and twirl me around like he did when he came home on leave. He'd never be able to play hide and seek or let me chase him in Honeycutt Park, letting me catch him. That night I learned how life could change with a snap of the fingers. I went to sleep and dreamed of my father dancing with me on the kitchen floor to Cold Play's music. He had a big grin on his face. But when I woke up, I choked back my sobs.

The next morning, I walked out to the kitchen and found Mom dressed in a gray suit, her hair pulled into a ponytail, stirring scrambled eggs on the stove. The smell of coffee lingered in the air as she served me sausage and eggs in our cheerful yellow kitchen. Only, there was nothing cheerful about the August day.

"Your father will be in the hospital for a while, so I've decided to put in for a transfer." She sat next to me and took a sip of coffee. "Now, Cassie, I know you're not going to want to hear this but, honey, we really need the money. We're going to have to move out of this expensive apartment and up to New Netherlands, Michigan to be closer to your grandparents because I will have some overnight travel. Anyway, I hear rent is lower there."

"Can't we cut out coupons and buy cheap food? I promise I won't eat much." I was determined to see if there was any way we could stay in North Carolina. I didn't want to leave my friends. Being an only child, my friends were important to me.

"No, we need a lot more than that." She put down her coffee mug and turned her full attention toward me. Her eyes searched my face. Mom scared me when she got that serious, as if I would have the answer to some big problem. "Here's the thing. I'm going to be traveling a lot, on the road."

I pushed out my lower lip.

"Now wait a minute," said Mom.

"I would have to go to another school."

"It's temporary. This job means I'll be traveling more, so I will be needing your grandparents to watch you from time to time."

She buttered a piece of toast and placed it on my plate. "I found a furnished apartment close to your grandparents. We can try it out and see how it works." She flipped open her computer to reveal a website. "See, isn't this cute?"

We were already living in our second apartment and nothing looked cute right now.

"B-but, M-m-m-mom." I caught myself before I went any further, but it was too late.

"Stop that stuttering. I mean it. Your teacher said you do that for attention, and I don't need any other stresses right now."

I dug my nails into the palms of my hands until I saw blood come out of the scratches. I'd learned it wasn't worth it to argue with Mom. It made things worse. Instead I went back to my bedroom where my pug, Snoozy, was napping and flung myself on the bed. Snoozy yawned and waddled up to my face, licked the tears from my cheeks, and snuggled into my arms. The thought of my father being in a wheelchair made me sad. It was worse than my Opa, grandpa, in Michigan. He uses a walker, and he's in his seventies. But I needed to be brave. It was part of being in a military family. We all knew to be strong, even though I wasn't feeling particularly strong right now. I felt wobbly, like one of those grocery carts with one wheel out of alignment.

In a week, we packed up our belongings, and Mom and I drove most of them to Cheapee Storage. "We'll be back for them soon," she promised me after stowing Christmas decorations, photo albums, knickknacks, and books. With the trunk and back seat packed with our clothes, my favorite stuffed penguin, and Mom's jewelry, we set out for New Netherlands, Michigan, a day and a half from our house. Snoozy panted in the back seat. He hated road trips, and this would be a long one. If I had been in a better mood, I would have enjoyed the thick woods and scattered lakes we passed on the way up north. But my bottom hurt from the long ride and my vision blurred as I thought how I would miss my friends back home. Moving to Michigan might as well have been moving to the Himalayas. Both were cold and scary.

We arrived in New Netherlands at about nine at night. Mom pulled onto Eighth Street and parked the car. The street was lined with two-story buildings with living quarters on the second floor and shops on the first floor. Oma, my grandma, said it reminded her of the old country. Shoppers stopped to admire window dressings or to stop in for an afternoon snack at Eet Smakelijk Bakery. The furnished apartment we'd be renting was above Kit-Kat Toys and only a block from my grandparents. It took four trips before we emptied the car. Snoozy huffed and puffed behind us like a good pug.

I walked into the main living room area, which had twelve-foot ceilings, white plush throw rugs, and sleek modern gray leather furniture that looked like it had just rolled off of a movie set. It was one of those magazine-type places that look like no one really lives there. Very fancy. Still, I missed our crummy old brown couch and oak rocking chair that had been friends for a long time.

"Wish we could have our old furniture."

"I know. Now you be careful with the furniture. We need to take care of it, or they'll ding us on the rent." She plunked down a box of kitchen supplies on top of the granite countertop and peeked at me through the opening between the counter and cabinets, her animated eyes not fooling me. "I'll whip up some of your favorite pancakes."

"Yes." I sighed and knew that meant we were out of money. Pancakes for dinner told me Mom probably had only a few dollars left in her checking account. The small amount my dad earned from his Army pay and Mom's job never seemed to be enough. I peered into one of the boxes and found two forks and knives and two plates. I set them down on the round glass table in the eating nook and found glasses, which I filled with water. I wondered if she'd found the syrup. I hated dry pancakes. I wondered if we'd have a stretch of dry food. The pantry didn't look too promising.

# —Chapter Two—

## New Netherlands

Well, even though I missed good old North Carolina, I was glad to be out of Fayetteville for the end of summer. Unlike the South, where the humid temperatures would drench your hair and clothes within five minutes of stepping outside into 80 percent humidity, Michigan summers treated its citizens kinder. My hair stayed straight and smooth for the first August of my life. I opened the front door and sucked in all the glorious air, a combination of summer flowers, lake smells, and scents from the nearby bakery. I stood on the threshold as summer wrapped its gentle arms around me. It almost made me not miss home, and I was amazed that summer could feel so good.

My stomach growled, and I realized I'd overslept. Ten o'clock, and I hadn't had my bowl of cereal. Mom said I was a creature of habit, and it was probably true. I had to have my Cocoa Krunchies each morning. I yanked a box out of the pantry just as the kitchen phone rang.

"Dearie, checking in to see how you're doing. Would you like to come have lunch with us? We're right down the street, a hop, skip, and a jump." Only my Oma could use such funny expressions. If I had hopped, skipped, and jumped, I would only reach our mailbox. I could hardly wait to see my grandparents.

"That would be great. Mom hasn't been to the grocery store yet."

"Cream of mushroom?"

"My favorite."

After I put my clothes away in the dresser drawer, I made my bed, smoothing out the black-and-white checked cover. What a weird room with everything covered in black and white. It was so boring. I walked back to the living room and punched the remote for the enormous big-screen TV, so much bigger than our 24-inch screen television that only got a few channels. I never dreamed there could be 233 channels. Wow! I watched a baking show about kids making cakes that looked like skyscrapers before I headed down the stairs to my bike. I was happy Oma and Opa lived nearby. It was scary staying in a new house with no one to talk to, not that Opa had much to say and Oma mainly asked if I was eating healthy and by the way, would I like a second cupcake? Only she could say two contradictory things in the same breath.

Oma sat on her balcony on the second story above the hardware store and waved. I locked my bike up next to a big tree. It had come from North Carolina, strapped onto the top of Mom's van, and thankfully stayed in one piece for the journey.

"Yoo-hoo!" She set aside the bowl of pole beans she'd been snapping and raced to the elevator, one of the cool things about their apartment. For seventy-three years old she could move pretty fast when she wanted to. Oma had had six kids, and Mom was the baby, so she came a lot later. Mom called herself the trailer. I wasn't sure what that meant but it had something to do with my aunts and uncles being a lot older than Mom.

"You poor dear." Oma's chubby arms squeezed me so tight I thought I'd pass out right there on the sidewalk. "So glad you're here, but my heart breaks for your daddy. Don't you worry, he's tough. Our boy will make it." She wiped away a tear that was headed into my ear. "Now come inside, Opa is crazy to see you." She mashed the button on the elevator, and we headed up.

The apartment was dark as Oma didn't like the sun shining in and fading her carpet or furniture. She was particular about those things. I stood in the hallway, adjusting to the low light and watching specks of dust float like summer snowflakes in the late morning rays while they landed on the gray-green carpet. A tall figure stood, his body outlined by what light streamed through the far kitchen window. "Hello, sweetie pie."

"Opa!" I rushed to him and leaned across his walker to give him a hug. I could smell the soap he used, the funny bars that curve in the middle and look like mint candy.

"My, you've grown. Must be all those sweet potatoes and nanner cream puddin' you've been eating down south."

I giggled. "I d-d-don't even l-l-like orange potatoes."

"No wonder you had to move north." He chuckled until it turned into a dry cough.

"Bob, you forgot to take your medicine." Oma rushed into the kitchen and came out, holding a cup of water and a pill. She lowered her brows and shot him a stern look.

"Oh, you worry too much, Edna." He took the cup and gulped down the water with his pill. "Now, where is that pack of Old Maid cards?"

We moved from the hallway to the living room off to the left. Oma pulled up the blinds, probably in celebration of my visiting, before going back to the kitchen to fix lunch. The room reminded me of summers when we'd come visit. The cream-colored sofa covered with a cheerful red flower pattern still had the striped afghan Oma knit a few summers ago. A couple of recliners faced a walnut coffee table. Opa maneuvered his walker so he could sit in one of the chairs and then motioned me to sit on the sofa. He removed the large vase in the center and plunked down the cards with the skill of a Las Vegas card shuffler. I loved watching him rip through the cards, and I loved the sound, too, as they flew through his thumbs at rapid speed.

"So, what has your mom said to you about your dad?" He arranged his cards so that they fanned out in front of him.

"Poppi's going to be in the hospital a while."

"When you've lost two legs you need a lot of rehab. But he's in a good place. Walter Reed is the best. Been there myself after 'Nam."

Oma plopped a letter on the table. "Mail call. Now, Bob don't give her all the gory details about the Vietnam War. She's a little girl."

"Needs to know about life. Got caught in a punji trap in 'Nam. Hole in the ground filled with bamboo poles whittled into a point. Ripped my calf right open."

"That's enough, dear." Oma tightened her apron ties. "Who's winning?"

"No one yet. Only reason I brought it up is to show Cassie you can survive an injury. Your dad will make it."

At lunch I sank my crackers into the mushroom soup and told my grandparents about what Fayetteville had been like. School, friends, sports teams, that kind of stuff. Then when Oma brought out her oatmeal cookie cakes, I turned to my grandfather.

"Can I see where the punji trap hurt you?" I winced as he showed me a pale, five-inch scar that ran the length of his calf. I touched it. "Does it hurt?"

"No, but for years it stung like thunder. Real sensitive. But nothing like what your dad's going through."

I pursed my lips together, reminded of the terrible pain my dad was in. Suddenly, I didn't want any more cookies. "I pray for Poppi every night."

"I'm sure you do, honey." His large bony hand reached out and enclosed mine. "The good Lord saved him, so you could still have a daddy."

# —Chapter Three—

## Ugly Shoes

The bus driver opened the big door, and I stepped down into my new world. After first heading down the wrong hallway, I dragged my feet into the strange classroom as thirty-two pairs of eyes followed me up to the teacher's desk.

"Class, we have a new student this year, Cassie Sanders." I tried to smile but my lips wouldn't cooperate and turn up. All I could think about was how my short black hair stood out in a sea of blond heads. Yes, there were a couple of dark-haired kids but most of the kids were of Dutch descent, with blue eyes and golden hair. And then there were the shoes. I peered down at my grubby tennis shoes and compared them with all the pairs of dainty girl's sandals planted on the floor in front of their desks. I stuck out like an elephant at a ballet class. *Oh, why didn't I wear something different?*

I found a seat next to the window and looked out at the pouring rain. Well, at least there would be inside recess, and I wouldn't have to sit by myself on an outside bench. It seemed weird to have such cold rain so early and the girls wearing sandals. It was still summer in Fayetteville. Back there, after the first day of school, my mom would take me and my friends to the city swimming pool down the street from my old house. I closed my eyes and imagined lying on my flamingo float, staring up at the slow-drifting clouds that lived in the Carolina blue sky. I could almost feel the leftover splashes made by kids doing cannonballs off the side of the pool.

The rest of the day dragged by until I jumped off the bus and ran upstairs to our apartment.

Mom was home early. "How was your day?"

"Okay."

"It takes time, honey."

"I need sandals. I was the only girl with shoelaces."

My mother chuckled. "Next paycheck."

"How's Poppi?" Mom had planned to call his hospital room at noon. I wanted so much to hear his voice.

"He was asleep for most of the time, but he did finally wake up. He said he misses you so much. He still has bandages around his knees, and they won't be able to do much until they heal. And he's drugged up with pain killers. Can't hardly talk."

Tears blurred my eyes as I listened to my mother's detailed report. He was so far away, he might as well be overseas.

"He said, 'Tell my baby girl to be strong and courageous. Look for a golden moment.'" She sighed and pulled a few cans of soup out of a plastic bag and set them on a high shelf in one of the cabinets. "Your dad is such an idealist. From where I sit, there are no golden moments in life." She frowned at me and then the finger came out. She loved to aim that at me. "The sooner you learn that, the less life will knock you down, hear me?"

"Yes, m-m-ma'am." But I knew she was wrong. Snoozy wagged his tail like he could read my thoughts and agreed with me.

"We'll make the best of being here." She finished unpacking the rest of the groceries, shoved the milk into the fridge, and edged onto one of the chrome stools next to me. "Tell you what, this weekend we'll check out some stores and see if they have any sandals left over from the summer. But I do think it's odd to wear sandals in this weather." She shook her head, her hoop earrings dancing madly. "Hope you'll make it with these northerners. I grew up here, so I know what to expect. Cassie, just try to fit in, okay?" Her serious look told me she meant business.

"Yes, ma'am."

The next Monday, I showed up at school with the cutest little brown sandals with turquoise tassels on top. Mom said they'd put a skip in my step. Maybe now I would fit in and make some friends. But no one noticed my new shoes, and when lunch period came, I found myself sitting alone again. I opened my shiny red vinyl lunch bag and pulled out a droopy tuna fish sandwich. It had limp lettuce sliding out of the sides, kinda like it was too tired to stay in the sandwich. I let out a groan. Again? Mom must have found another great deal on tuna. Lucky me.

"Oh, my favorite sandwich. Can I sit with you?" I looked up to see a girl from class staring at me. Her round eyes peered through dark eyeglass frames, scrutinizing me. She giggled, as her tight black curls bounced. "Talk southern to me."

"Pardon?"

"You know, say something like, "I love hush puppies and grits, y'all."

"I, I don't kn-n-now what ..."

"Oh, forget it." She pulled out a brown paper bag with a large "Marie Louise" printed in block letters. "Mom makes up our lunches and makes sure we all get the right bag."

"How many kids in your f-f-f-f-family?" I bit my tongue and cursed my stupid brain. Why couldn't I talk normally?

"Six. I'm the second from the bottom. I have four brothers and a baby sister. All we talk about around the dinner table is football. Football, football, football. It's awesome." I glanced at her and noticed her pants had grass stains on them. I wondered if she practiced football with her brothers. She noticed me staring at her knees. "Yep, Mom keeps yelling at me because I ruin my jeans. Plus, since I'm small for my age, she says to me, 'Honey, don't ya want to sit down and play a nice quiet video game?' Booring. I was the smallest in class until you moved here. Say, you want that whole sandwich?" She smiled and a tiny dimple sprouted in her left cheek.

"You can have it. I eat tuna fish sandwiches so much that I'm growing fins."

She sat across from me at the round table and passed me half of a turkey sandwich and two Oreo cookies, the only dessert she had. That's when I knew I had a friend. Nobody would ever give away their best treat. Marie Louise would help me make it through fifth grade.

I found out she liked drawing, soft-serve ice cream, and scary movies. She also hated Austin Alexander, the smartest boy in school. "He's thinks he's the best soccer player in school, and his uncle is the mayor." I liked how she scrunched up her nose at the mention of him. "How come you're new here?" she asked as she wadded up her lunch bag and pitched it into the plastic trash can.

"Oh, Mom's working ... she has to travel for her job, and my dad's … well, he's in another state getting some help with his legs."

"Well, hope it works out. Legs come in handy." She giggled until she saw the look on my face. I was trying hard not to let tears escape, but a couple of them did anyway. I was trying to be brave like Poppi had asked, but it wasn't working well.

"I'm sorry, I didn't mean to hurt your feelings." She gave me a big hug, and I knew I had a buddy.

"The mailman brought you a letter," said Oma as she walked in the front door, waving an envelope with my father's loopy handwriting. She handed it to me, and I ran to my bedroom. Flopping onto my bed, I ripped open the letter.

Dear sweet Cassie,

Oh, how I miss you. The days are long as I lie in this bed trying to get my life back. I have so much to be thankful for. I'm alive and I have the most precious daughter in the world.

I hope school is going well. I know you are a great speller and Grandma says you might be able to be in the school spelling bee. That's great. Don't neglect learning fractions, they are important!

My days are long but I'm not complaining. I first have doctor rounds where my doctor checks on me to see if my meds are okay and to see if I have any infections. My arm is healing up nicely and I have a bunch of stuffing up my nose and a big bandage over it. I look like a clown, maybe I can join a circus when I get out of here.

I have a nice nurse named Christine who pushes me to my appointments in my wheelchair. Yes, I do have a wheelchair and

I'm glad to have some "wheels" to get around, hopefully I will be able to purchase a motorized one down the road. I have physical therapy in the morning but not much happening in the afternoon, so the days are long.

I pray for you and your mother. I will be here several months, and it won't be easy for any of us. Life is hard sometimes, but we need to stay in the fight, don't we?

When I got hit and was lying on the dirt floor in Afghanistan, I kept picturing you as a little baby with your hands out for me to pick you up. I kept thinking I have to survive this thing, my daughter needs me. So, I will try hard to do what the doctors say and work hard to learn to use my different body. I'm asking you to be strong and courageous. Look for someone needier than yourself and help them. That's your calling—to find a golden moment. I promise if you find someone to help, it will make you happy.

Love, Poppi

I put his letter away in a special purple-flowered box with a picture of Elsa from *Frozen* on top that I kept in the top drawer of my bureau and looked at the framed photo of my parents that my mother had given to me before she started working. I missed my tall, dark-haired father. I figured he wouldn't be tall anymore. I might be taller than him without his legs. I hoped his new legs would still make him tall. I thought about what he said about finding someone needy to help. I didn't know anyone needy except maybe me. But I decided to what Poppi called "ponder."

"Pondering is an important thing in life," he told me a year ago, when he had come home on leave and was putting me to bed. He had just read me *The Giving Tree*. He looked me straight in the eye and said, "Cassie, too many people don't take time to ponder, and because of that, the important, deep mysteries of life slip by. We've got a whole country of people who don't pay attention. Don't you be that way." I remembered the serious look in his eyes as he peered down at me snuggled deep in my bed. My head bobbed up and down as I nodded in agreement. I would do anything for Poppi.

# —Chapter Four—

## *Who Tripped Me?*

My feet went out from under me as I fell on my back, the ground reaching up to touch me with a splat. I lay there catching my breath and inhaling the crisp October air.

"Looks kinda like an upside-down bug that just got exterminated."

I stretched out my feet on the ground, remembering a strange leg had blocked my path. After I caught my breath, I looked up, shading my eyes from the noon sun. A tall, skinny boy loomed above. He had short, spiky hair that looked like a pile of hay had exploded on top of his head and a ruddy face that suggested he should never stay in the sun too long. He glared at me, scorn dripping from his face. Who was this annoying creature from the other team?

"I-I-I tripped. I mean, y-y-you t-t-t-tripped me."

"Only one 't' in trip." He turned around and looked at his team behind him, his palms facing skyward as if to say, "*Hey, I haven't a clue as to how this happened.*"

"Jerk," I muttered under my breath. I squeezed my eyelids together, so I wouldn't cry. When I opened them, he put out a hand, but I waved it away.

Marie Louise flew to my side from mid-field, her cocoa-brown face dipped in sweat, and very angry. She stopped, reared back, and kicked the guy in the shin. "Hey, Noah, I saw that."

He yelped and rubbed his leg. "You got one heck of a kick, Tuttle."

I pushed up with my arms and came into a standing position but not before Miss Hathaway showed up, her whistle shrill and piercing. "You three get back in the game. I don't know what happened, but we don't have all day to visit here."

"But, Miss Hathaway," said Marie Louise.

"What?" She looked at the three of us and blew a piece of trailing hair out of her face.

"He tripped Cassie."

"Noah?"

Noah pursed his lips together. His mouth looked like a couple of smashed worms, his eyes, two lit firecrackers. I could see he was planning a good one. "Hey, can I help it if she can't run?"

"So not true," blurted my new best friend.

"You two will have to take a trip to the principal's office. Seems to me the best way to sort this out is to make a quick call to your parents."

That night my mother was in a mood. I could tell because she was slamming pots and pans around while water for the spaghetti boiled. I sat on one of the stools, watching the whole show. I wasn't scared. She just has those moods, and I don't take it personally anymore. Better than her sad moods.

"M-m-mom, I didn't do anything. He t-t-tripped me. Honest." I wanted to press my case because that Noah seemed to be out to get me.

"That's not what he said. He said you ran into him, and then when you fell, you started screaming at him."

"Not true. Not true. M-m-mom, believe me." I spat out the words. I couldn't believe she was taking Noah's side.

"Well, I didn't see the kid, but I'm telling you, I don't want any trouble in this town. We wouldn't be here if we didn't have to. I left ten years ago and never thought I'd step foot in this sanctimonious town again." She turned off the faucet and wiped her hand on a towel with such vehemence that I thought she'd pull the skin off her hands.

I hadn't seen the word sanctimonious on my spelling test yet but decided it was safer to look it up than ask. Instead I said, "Mom, why did you leave?"

My mom, her back still to me, drained the spaghetti into a large bowl and banged it down on our kitchen table. "Not for you to ask." She shook her head and went back to the kitchen for the tossed salad.

"Well, it's an okay place for me."

"Yes, three seasons here. Waiting for snow, watching it snow, and cleaning up the snow. Oh yeah, and six weeks of summer."

"Well, at least I have Opa and Oma."

Mom brought two empty plates to the table. "Come eat." I slid off the stool.

"How about grace?" I asked.

"Suit yourself." She popped a forkful of spaghetti Bolognese into her mouth, but then dropped her utensil. "Hey, I'm sorry, Cassie. I had a bad day at work. Burger Hut canceled my biggest order, and I needed part of that for next month's rent. Sometimes I wish I could get a break, especially with your father across country in rehab."

"A lot could ch-ch-change in twenty-four hours, Mom." I took my fingers and tried to push the sides of my mouth up in an exaggerated grin to make her laugh. "Poppi says that."

"Your dad is an eternal optimist." She picked up her phone to check her text messages. "Hope he'll call tonight. Say, let's FaceTime him. We won't say anything about the fight."

"Okay, but I didn't start it."

"Whatever." She picked up her plate and put it in the sink. Discussing the fight was over.

# —Chapter Five—

## *Class Projects*

Miss Hathaway clapped her hands together in a little rhythm, and we knew that was her way of getting our class's attention. I liked watching her get excited. Her blue eyes grew larger, and her wide mouth created a perfect "O." And her hair, light brown and smooth, would bounce and catch the overhead light as she talked. Her clapping usually meant some big announcement. "Children, since it's November, and the holidays are coming up, I would like for all of you to think about a service project you might do this season. This will be for half of your Citizenship grade. I will give you a few days to figure out your plan, and then you will be writing down, in essay form, what you will do."

Jessimyn raised her hand. "I sing in the choir at church. I think that's very giving." Her ruddy face wore the pleased look of someone who had already figured out how to get on the best side of her teacher.

"Big whoop," said Sam Van Dyke. He had the best surfer hair in the fifth grade and was best friends with Noah Huizenga, who had tripped me during the soccer game. Much to my horror, he and Noah just transferred into our class. Rumor was that even though it was Miss Hathaway's first year of teaching, she was the best teacher at handling mouthy fifth-grade boys. Lucky me. He sat on one side of me with Jessimyn on the other. As much as I didn't want to sit with Noah, I *really* didn't want to sit next to Jessimyn. She talked all the time. Especially about church. I thought she was too heavenly to live on earth. She liked to trumpet all of her good deeds she did for Jesus. I kind of felt sorry for Jesus having to listen to all her accomplishments. I didn't have anything against Jesus. No, sir. I love him too, but you shouldn't think you should brag about how much you work for him.

"You're one to talk, Sam. I'll bet you never did anything for anyone anyway," said Jessimyn. "Anyway, it says 'blessed are those who serve the Lord.'"

Miss Hathaway looked flustered and told them both to be quiet. Since it was her first year of teaching, I sure didn't want her to give up. I kind of felt sorry for her. She'd start out each day standing in front of the class with a smile as she wrote a happy quotation on the board. But by the end of the day, she slumped at her desk, watching the clock for the exact moment she could dismiss us for the bus. I decided right then and there I'd never be a fifth-grade teacher. I think I'd rather work at a zoo feeding alligators than put up with some of the brats in my class.

Marie Louise saved me a place in line for the bus. Even though we lived close to school, we took the bus on really cold days. "I know what I'm going to do for my class project." She wore a tiny smile that threatened to grow large if she didn't say something soon.

"What?"

"I have a new cupcake kit I got for my birthday. I thought I could make everyone in our class a cupcake with their birthday written in icing on top."

I frowned. "Aren't we supposed to help people outside of our class?"

She sighed. "You're right. Maybe I could have a cupcake booth in front of my house and earn money for the Red Cross." I reminded her that we already had two inches of snow on the ground and it would only be getting worse. How could she have a cupcake booth in winter?

"Guess I didn't think of that. I just love to bake."

"That's okay, you'll think of something brilliant, I know."

"Do you have any ideas?"

I frowned. "I-I don't know anyone I could h-h-help except my grandparents and the teacher said that doesn't c-c-count." I pulled my hat down further on my head as the crisp winter wind blasted everyone in line. "I'm going to ponder it like my daddy says to do."

When the bus stopped at my corner, I walked down the bus steps.

"Don't forget to ponder tonight," she said and gestured to me our secret signal, two forefingers linked together. I did it back to her.

"Mom!" I hollered as I walked through the front door of my grandparents' apartment. I had been living there while she was on the road, and she was home today. Her black hair hit right above her shoulders. She was still wearing her working clothes—black pants, blazer, her bangle bracelets, and the large string of pearls she said brought her luck. It had been three weeks since I had seen her last, and I missed her terribly. Some nights she'd call. Other nights, nobody could get a hold of her.

She squeezed me in a bear hug. "Oh, I missed you, sweetie." I smelled her perfume, something called Hawaiian Sunset, and for a moment, all was right with the world.

Suddenly, I remembered how hard I tried to call her last night. "W-w-why didn't you a-a-answer your phone?" I pulled back from her, crossing my arms to show my indignation.

"Oh, you know how busy I am on the road. I had a client I had to show a style of restaurant booth, and we ended up having dinner at the restaurant. I guess I didn't hear your ring."

"It's okay."

"Sit down on the sofa, and we'll catch up." She patted a place next to her. I plopped down. "Your grandparents left some groceries. I told them I'd make Swedish meatballs for dinner here."

I was surprised as Mom didn't cook a lot. She worked late some nights and brought home takeout: burgers, Chinese beef and broccoli, or Taco Bell. I listened half-heartedly as she described the recipe, something she'd picked up at one of the restaurants she'd called on.

"The trick to this is in the sauce. You need to season it with nutmeg and then add the sour cream at the last minute." To listen to her you'd think it was the most gourmet recipe in the universe, not just clumps of ground meat rolled into balls with some fancy sauce. I really didn't want to hear about the restaurants she visited, trying to sell them furniture and all the wonderful food she ate, but I nodded in all the right places.

Finally, she took a breath, and I started in. "Poppi sent me a letter. Want to read it?"

"That's okay, sweetie, just tell me what it said." She looked into the distance like she was trying not to let her emotions get the best of her, then back at me, her gray-blue eyes blinking to keep tears at bay.

"Well, he s-s-said he was in a wheelchair and that he has physical ther … ther … therapy. He has a nice nurse, Christine, who pushes him up and down the corridors and takes him to appointments."

"He'll be there for several months until he stabilizes. Then they'll transfer him to Mary Free Bed in Grand Rapids where he'll learn how to function with his new legs. It will still be difficult for him to do things he did before."

"Like what?"

"Well, for example, he won't be able to be a roofer anymore. He'll have to train for another career when he's discharged." My mind spun with all kinds of worries. How would he earn a living? How could he put on shoes? Would he wear socks? How could he get around the house or drive a car? My mother must have seen my worried look. She took my hands in hers and looked at me. I fingered her wedding ring. "No, don't you worry about him. We talked, and he's going to be fine." She pulled her hands away and ruffled my hair. "Now you wash your hands. You and I are going to make dinner. Opa and Oma will be home in a minute." And before I could blink, she was in the kitchen chopping onions. Mom could swish away a problem and walk away to start a new project.

But I still worried about my father. Even as I chopped tomatoes for salad, I wondered what he was having for dinner. Did the hospital feed him enough? He had a habit of going back for seconds and finished the evening off with a big bowl of ice cream, but from what Mom told me, the hospital only gives people a miniature round cardboard container of the frozen stuff and then you have to eat it with a flat wooden spoon, the kind that gives me the shivers. I didn't want him to become skinny and sad.

After dinner, I read my letter from Poppi, and Oma tucked me in bed after reading me two chapters from *On the Banks of Plum Creek*. She sat down on my bed next to me, her rose cologne drifting into my nose as I closed my eyes and imagined living in the

1800s on the prairie. Then my thoughts came back to Dad.

"Oma, do you think Mom will be able to see Poppi soon? I hope they are feeding him enough food. Is he in a lot of pain?"

Oma put her finger to her mouth. "Shhh … so much worry for such a little girl. It's an excellent hospital, and he's in good care." She was like her daughter, Mom, who never wanted to talk about serious matters. They probably didn't want me to worry. She handed me my stuffed penguin, smoothed my blankets, and tucked them into the side of the bed before saying prayers and kissing me good night.

When she left, I lay in bed tossing and turning as I heard the three of them talk in hushed tones. Straining my ears, I heard words like "separation," "VA hospital," "prosthetics," and "income." Try as I would, I couldn't put the words together to make sense. Instead, I closed my eyes, trying to be brave even though tears dotted my pillow. All I wanted was to see Poppi again.

# —Chapter Six—

## Stomach Ache

A blur of faces, most with blue eyes and straw-colored hair, stared at me as I stood in front of the class, still unfriendly after three months. I would rather do five pages of my math workbook than stand up in front of my classmates. I had made a friend of Marie Louise, and sometimes Eric Fuller, the kid who had a long skinny face, and would pick me for a spelling partner. He had a buzz cut and a habit of squinting his brown eyes.

Miss Hathaway stood in front of her desk in the front corner of the room. "Now, class, as it's November 12th, I've asked you all to report your plans for your community service projects. Cassie will start us off. Cassie…"

"Umm, well, I thought I might take care of our neighbors' pet rabbit when they are gone for Christmas." Even as the words left my mouth, they sounded silly and unimportant. It wasn't noble or magnificent. It sounded more like a Saturday morning chore. My hands felt sweaty as I felt a room full of eyes drill into me. Had I said something wrong?

"Well, that's a nice gesture, Cassie." She put her hands together and pressed them to her mouth to make a point. "I think the goal of our project is to do something more … well, more community service." I knew by her kind eyes that she didn't mean to embarrass me, but right then I wanted to crawl into my desk and stay there until everyone left for the day. Couldn't she see Sam snickering and his sidekick pulling his legs up to his stomach and putting his hands up like bunny ears? Or Jessimyn, her brow lowered, planning to criticize my plan. It was hard to listen to the other students' plans of selling homemade jewelry to donate to homeless animal shelters, creating a recycling center for the library, and starting a reading program for underprivileged preschoolers.

I didn't feel much better at lunch, which sat heavy in my stomach before sliding up my throat. I held my mouth, raced out the door to the girls' restroom, and found a stall. I leaned over the bowl, heaved until nothing was left, and then leaned against the wall. I needed to get back to class as lunch was over, and I didn't want to be late.

"I did the same thing my first day here." A pair of dark trousers with loafers appeared below the stall's door. Miss Hathaway? How did she know where I was?

"You did?"

"Yep. Not easy to be new in school, even for teachers."

Flushing the toilet, I stood and pushed open the door. "Don't tell anyone."

"Only if you don't tell anyone about me." She took my arm and led me to the sink. With a moist paper towel, she wiped off my face and smoothed my hair back. "Take a few minutes to find your composure and come back to class." She winked at me. Suddenly

I realized we had a secret bond—we both had nervous stomachs.

"So how was school?" my grandmother asked that afternoon. She'd had one of her sick days, and I was bringing her tea in bed. The room hadn't changed for years, with its pink floral bedspread and pale-gray striped wallpaper. She sat propped up in bed, reading a romance novel.

"Can't I just move back to my old school? I don't like this one."

My grandmother picked up the steaming mug of tea and stirred it. "I thought things were going well with you. Don't you have a new friend, Marie Louise? You should try and bring her around sometime."

"It's not that. Marie Louise is very nice. It's just I don't fit in." I flipped on her bedside lamp as dusk was seeping, sneaky and dull, into the day's end. Winter up north had a way of stealing the day before a person was ready to give it up.

"I'm sure it will work out." She pointed to the delicate wood side chair with the needlepointed seat and motioned me to sit. "I have something else I need to say." She stirred her tea, clinking the spoon against the side of the cup.

I slid my bottom onto the chair. "What, Oma?"

She stirred some more as if the stirring might help her locate the correct words. "You know your mother is very busy working. She has a lot of travel for this job and wants to make sure she keeps it. She doesn't know when your father will finish his rehab, so she's trying to pile up money while she can." She put the cup to her lips and sipped. "Now I need you to be very grown up about my next statement." She caught my eyes and held them. "You will have to stay here for the rest of the school year and maybe longer. So, I hope you will settle in and make the best of it." She glanced at Snoozy, curled up on the floor beside the bed. "And don't forget to feed him. He looks hungry."

Snoozy started to pant hard at the word "feed," and his saliva dripped into a puddle on the floor.

Probably now wasn't the best time to tell her I was sick in school. I loved my grandmother, but I'm sure she couldn't remember what it was like to be in fifth grade. The last thing I wanted was to worry her. Instead I said, "Yes, Oma. How about some hand lotion?" I popped the lid on her favorite lavender cream and poured a dab into the palms of her hands.

She smiled. "Such a thoughtful child. Now go and turn on the oven so we can heat up the casserole. It will be the last night before your mother leaves."

"She didn't tell me that. Why does she have to go so soon?" Mom had only been back for two days.

I trotted into the kitchen and turned the dial on the oven. When it beeped, I went to the refrigerator and pulled out the round glass dish filled with leftover chicken stew and slid it onto a rack.

"Can you break up some of that lettuce for a salad?" Oma called from the other room.

"Sure." I was thankful I had a chore to keep me busy, so I wouldn't be thinking about Mom going away or the embarrassing day I had at school.

Mom showed up an hour later, and during dinner, as Mom entertained us with her stories about clients, I decided I'd tell her tomorrow about my terrible day. I thought about my dad's words in his letter. "Look for the golden moments in life."

I still didn't know what he meant by that.

# —Chapter Seven—

*Scrabble*

The next day I asked Oma if I could walk to school as it was only two blocks away.

"All right, but don't talk to Mr. Jacob. He's in a bad mood today."

I slid my backpack on and walked down the outdoor stairs of my grandparents' apartment. They lived above Mr. Jacob's hardware store. He wore blue denim overalls and leaned on a cane, which he used to punctuate his discussions with customers.

I scooted past the store so Mr. Jacob wouldn't quiz me about why I wasn't taking the school bus and if my coat was warm enough. Today when I passed by, he was out shoveling his walkway in his gray plaid coat and the funny hat with long flaps that covered his ears. He waved his shovel in the air as I started to pass in front of him. My heart raced. The last thing I wanted to do was to talk to this strange man who smelled of smoke and fried onions.

"Hey, you the kid who leaves candy bar papers in front of my door?" I stopped, but I didn't want to say anything to him. "Did you hear me, girl?"

"What?"

His words were garbled, but his look wasn't. His eyes narrowed so low that his eyebrows almost met. I was so fascinated with them I didn't answer.

"Hey, you, yeah, I'm talking to you." A long, hairy finger pointed at me, and I stepped back.

"I'm sorry, no, I didn't."

"Well, make sure your little friends don't litter in front of my store. I've got enough to do without chasing down trash." He turned on his heels and headed back into the store, the bell on the back of the door clanging while it closed.

I raced to Marie Louise's house, wanting to put some distance between him and me. My friend lived in a gray two-story house on White Tail Street, about three blocks away. She waited on the porch and waved. As we headed south, I told her about my encounter with our neighbor. "He's creepy," I told Marie Louise.

"My mom says he's mean because he hardly has any customers anymore. I think he scares everyone off. Anyway, everyone orders on the internet if they need anything."

"Oh, I don't want to talk about that old guy," I said. We walked in silence for a few minutes; the only sounds were the city bus passing us and a late Canadian goose honking in the sky. He must have missed his flock when they left in October for warmer parts. A break in the clouds gave the sun permission to shine for a few short moments, and it reminded me of something. I turned to my friend, who had stuffed her hands in her coat pockets to keep them warm. "Do you know what a golden moment is?"

"A what?" She scrunched up her face and tipped her head sideways like she did when she thought I had a crazy idea, which was a lot. But that was what I liked about Marie Louise. At least she listened to me.

"My dad says to look for golden moments, but I don't know where they are."

"They're probably in a bank vault or under a rainbow?" asked Marie Louise. "You know, rainbow, like in fairy tales."

"Nah, that's not what he meant." I pulled my winter hat down over my ears as an icy breeze swept past. "I think it's when the sun shines so hard on the water in the summer that it looks like little sparkly flecks of light."

"Yeah, that's it. But why would your dad think you could find it in winter?"

"Dunno."

"I hope he comes home soon."

"Me too."

Marie Louise sighed. "I don't know what I'd do if my dad lost his legs."

At morning break, Miss Hathaway let us go to different stations for math games, crafts, or word puzzles. I chose word puzzles because, well, I just like words. All kinds. Long ones, short ones, complicated ones, simple ones. I might not be good at saying them, but I sure like collecting them. This week's game was Scrabble, and I was pretty good at winning.

I almost decided to change stations when I saw Sam Van Dyke sit down next to me, but then I decided I could probably win and that would be fun to beat him. He was the most popular boy in the class, and he loved to comment about my shoes whenever he walked by me. *Man, I'd like to show this guy up.* His short blond hair was smooth with a dip in the front, and he had a way of running his hand over the dip when he wanted to call attention to himself—which seemed a lot.

We both picked a tile. "Okay," he said. "I'll start 'cause I have the letter 'a.'"

"Ch-ch-cheater, I have an 'a' too."

"Let's do rock, paper, scissors. The person who wins gets to start first."

Of course he won. He always won. He had a perfect life. Back and forth we set down the tiles until Sam leaped up, waving his hands in triumph. "I killed it ... ha, I killed it."

He had a goofy grin on his face, kinda like the look someone gets when they know they have something on the other guy. I looked down at the board and saw he had spelled out, "limp."

"Ah, can't ya take a little joke?" His mouth curled into a cruel imitation of a smile. "Get it? Everyone knows about your dad."

I clenched my teeth, not wanting to cry in front of the guy who was the class know-it-all. I felt the breath go out of me like I was going to faint, so I held on to the edge of the game table. My insides swelled up like I was a water balloon in summer, ready to burst, but I didn't say anything. It seemed like whenever I got in an argument, I was at loss for words. It's like an invisible hand comes along and zips up my mouth. My first thought was to run to the bathroom again, but I knew I'd be mocked even worse if I did that. I looked down at the table, not knowing what to do.

"What's going on over there?" Miss Hathaway asked. Sam took the board and jiggled it so no one could see what it spelled.

"I saw it." Jessimyn waved her hand wildly from the craft station. "He spelled limp."

"And what's wrong with that?"

Jessimyn rushed over to her teacher and whispered in her ear.

"I'm surprised at you, Jessimyn," Miss Hathaway said, in a tone that might have also said, "You forgot your lunch money again." I could tell she thought Jessimyn was making it up. "Is that true, Sam?"

"No."

She sent everyone back to their own desks and Jessimyn to the "thinking" corner, named so a student could spend some time there reforming their attitude. I could tell Miss Hathaway thought she was gossiping and making it all up. It was the first time

*Jessimyn* had to go think things over. I turned around and saw the whole class was trying not to smile as she slunk to the back corner of the room.

# —Chapter Eight—

## Story of the Red Kettle

"The mailman brought you a letter," Oma called from her bedroom when I came home from school. She'd had another sick day, which meant we'd probably have frozen pot pies for dinner. Actually, I loved those pies with the bright-green peas and creamy sauce. I wouldn't mind eating them every night.

I poked my head in the doorway of her room. All I could see was a little wisp of gray hair and her eyes peering out from the sheet. "I'll get you some hot tea. Where's the letter?"

"On the kitchen counter next to the sugar canister." Her voice sounded weaker than normal. I hoped Opa would be home soon from his dentist appointment.

I ran into the kitchen and filled up a coffee mug, the one with blue flowers. Oma loved anything with flowers. I slid it into the microwave and set the timer for one minute before picking up the long envelope with my father's familiar writing on it.

Dear Cassie,

I've been thinking about the school project that you wrote me about. I think your teacher, Miss Hathaway, is to be commended for having your class do some community service before Christmas. You and your fellow students are never too young to learn how to serve others. There are so many needy folks out there who could use a boost, not just financially but in all ways. Do you have any ideas? Time is slipping away, and it will soon be Christmas, so better get hustling! You and your mother and I have been so blessed to have a warm house, plenty of food, and a loving family, but nowadays that's rarer. I know you have a caring heart and will find the perfect project. Don't be afraid of any of the kids in class. Often the most insecure ones like to pick on someone new like you. Just forget about that old Sam and his friend, Noah!

I am doing more therapy every day. My physical therapist says I need to concentrate on strengthening my arms. They will have to substitute for my legs for any mobility until I get new ones. And when I do get fitted for my prosthetics—your scientific word for the day—especially my running ones, I will dance and spring up and down like a grasshopper.

I haven't heard much from your mother although she did FaceTime me last week. I'm sure she's busy making money to help with extra expenses.

Have you figured out a Golden Moment yet? I'm not going to tell you, you'll have to figure it out for yourself.

Make sure you wear a hat every day as it's now turning cold and don't forget to bring

your grandmother her tea when you get
home from school. I wish I could see you, but
maybe we can Skype this weekend.

All my love,
Poppi

I tucked my letter in with the other ones I had
been saving in my purple metal box with the picture
of Elsa on the top. I slid the drawer closed, and
suddenly I had an idea for my school project. On a
whim, I slipped back into Oma's room and dropped
onto the foot of her bed.

She sat up, taking a needlepoint pillow from
behind her and placing it on the chair next to the bed.
"Did you make tea?"

"Oops." I ran back to the kitchen and brought her
the steaming mug. Then I picked up a throw pillow
on her bed and examined it. "Oma, why does this
cushion with the red pot say, 'Keep the pot boiling'?"
Somewhere in the back of my mind I remembered
a story about the red kettle, but I wanted to hear it
again.

"Not now, dear, I'm tired. Maybe tomorrow." I
watched the thin, bluish eyelids close. "I'll be better
tomorrow. Tell Opa we will have pigs in a blanket
tonight. Heat them at three hundred and fifty degrees
for twenty minutes."

As I pulled the pigs out of the oven, Opa came through the front door, his shiny bald head catching the light in the hallway by the door. He used his cane, so he must be feeling better. Some days he could get around just fine without the walker.

We sat down to dinner, and I started to quiz him about his day. I don't think he likes going to the dentist, because he didn't say much. Then I paused. "Opa, tell me about the red pot on the needlepoint cushion. You know, the one on Oma's chair in the bedroom."

His eyes grew merry as he thought about it. "Your grandmother was one of the ringers. That's how I first met her."

"Ringer?" I took another bite of the pastry-wrapped sausage and swallowed. "Is that right?"

"Loved every minute of it," said Oma.

He unbuckled his belt one notch, a sign he'd enjoyed a meal. "She rang a bell for the Salvation Army."

"What's that? Something like the Army Poppi's in? And why did they have bells?" I was confused.

"It's a Christian service organization. They collect money for the poor, and would ring the bells to have people notice them." Opa got a distant look in his eye, and I knew he was about to tell a story. "You know,

I used to walk by every day on my way to work at the lumberyard in the month before Christmas in 1968. I dropped a quarter into your grandmother's kettle every day. It was taking a bit of a chunk out of my weekly earnings, but it was a chance to walk by this beautiful blonde-haired young lady with ruddy cheeks and talk to her. The moment I dropped my money in the kettle, she'd stop ringing her bell, and we'd talk."

"More like you talked and I listened," said Oma.

He chuckled at the memory. "Yes sir, she was pretty shy, so I kept the comments impersonal. Mostly, 'How's the weather been today?' or 'Have you collected much this week?' She'd blush and answer me in a few words. Then she'd smile and pick up her bell again. She was very conscientious."

"So, when did you finally spend time with her?"

"It was Christmas Eve, about seven at night. She stood outside of Harvey's Fine Groceries. Harvey was a kind man and kept checking to see if she needed coffee or a short rest inside of the store. Well, when she came in for break, I was still moseying around the store, wasting my time, waiting for her to show up. I saw her buy a cup of coffee at the soda fountain and head toward the magazine section. I went up to her and said, 'You shouldn't be walking home alone with all that loot. Let me accompany you.' Yes, sir, right while she was thumbing through a *Ladies Home Journal* magazine."

"I never knew that. Was Oma good at collecting money?"

"Good? Why, she was the top bell ringer. The Salvation Army depended a lot on their volunteers to bring in money to support their programs for the next year. Sometimes grandparents whose parents had lived through World War I told their grandkids about the Donut Girls. They were young women who volunteered to be on the front lines in Europe during the war. They spent their time mixing up dough and frying donuts in a little hut for the soldiers. Sometimes they fried the donuts in the soldier's helmets when they didn't have enough frying pans! Many soldiers never forgot them and made it a point to give money to the red kettles."

"They were b-b-brave. I mean, they could have got killed."

"Yes."

"So, I guess you saw her again."

"We had a whirlwind courtship because I was being shipped over to Viet Nam. On my first leave home, I came back and married her. The rest is history." He reached for another pig and squirted a large dollop of mustard on top. He loved mustard. Oma said Opa would put that yellow stuff on her apple crumb pie if she let him.

# —**Chapter Nine**—

*Letter to Poppi*

I thought about him and Oma when I brushed my teeth that night and when I kissed my grandparents goodnight. And, as I looked out at the cold half-moon whose rays decorated my bedroom's windowsill, I hatched a plan.

The next morning, I stayed in at recess after the bell rang. I waited at my desk while Miss Hathaway sat at her desk grading papers.

She finally looked up. "What's up, Cassie?" She smiled and turned back to her papers.

"M-m-may I talk to you a minute?"

"Why, of course."

I walked up to her desk and stood on one foot and then the other as the words came out, fighting themselves for the right order. "I, w-w-well, maybe it might be a g-g-good idea, that is if you think s-s-s-so, for my community project to become a bell ringer."

"I didn't think the community clock tower had musicians anymore to pull the ropes. It's automated."

"No, a b-b-b-bellringer like those who have red kettles."

She smiled and showed her dimples. "Oh, that kind." Then she frowned, and I wasn't sure why. Sure seemed like a good idea to me.

"Do they still do that? Isn't all that stuff online?"

I didn't know what to say. She must have sensed my discomfort because she reached out for my hand and gave it a squeeze. "I don't know why that can't work out. Let me run it by Principal Van Ark and see what he says." It seemed odd that she had to discuss the topic with the principal, but she nodded like the principal would okay it.

Right after recess and before Social Studies, Miss Hathaway stopped me at her desk for a minute. Her face told me trouble was brewing.

"I don't know how to say this, but I'm afraid our school administration is wary about sanctioning any religious projects for the holidays."

I didn't know what sanctioning meant but it didn't sound good. "But it's, w-w-well, you k-k-know, Christmas, that's why we are doing community projects." I shocked myself by blurting out the words. Miss Hathaway leaned her head into the palm of her right hand like she had a headache and wanted to be anywhere rather than talking to me about my project. She stood, pushed away from the chair, and paced back and forth behind her desk. Then she stopped. "Cassie, I do think it's a great idea. Tell you what, I'll okay the project, and if there's any problem, let me take care of it. I think you have a large heart, and I want to encourage you."

She looked straight at me, her pink painted lips turning up into a bright smile, shiny like. The smile kept me warm all the way home.

That night after doing dishes, I wrote a letter to my dad. I wanted him to know I was being courageous, in my own little corner of the world, like he was in his.

Dear Poppi,

I hope your rehab is doing well and that you can come home soon. Mom came by last week. I don't see her much, so I guess that means she is working hard to help make ends meet. I wish she didn't have to travel so much. I like Opa and Oma, but they are pretty old. Still, Oma cooks good dinners and Opa checks my homework. I hate fractions, but I think I'm starting to figure them out.

Everyone in class is supposed to do a community project for the Christmas season and guess what I picked? I am going to be a bell ringer for the Salvation Army. I am so excited. I want to help poor people during Christmas, and I will be just like Oma. Miss Hathaway said I need to have adult supervision so Oma or Opa will check on me, or Mr. Jacob or Mrs. Huizenga downstairs. No one would ever mess with Mr. Jacob and his cane.

I'm trying to be brave like you are. I miss you so much. Sending you lots of kisses.

Love,
Cassie.


I decorated it with a couple of Dad's favorite stickers, an eagle and an American flag, and stuck it in the envelope. I put the letter on the top of my chest of drawers next to the picture of him. Poppi was in his Army uniform and had his arm around Mom and me. It was right before he went back to Afghanistan for his last tour of duty. His solemn, brown eyes peered out from his hat, barely covering his brown, curly hair. Mom didn't look quite as happy. Her mouth barely turned up in a half smile and her eyes had a faraway look. I figured it was probably because she knew he was going away again.

The next day, Opa took me to the Salvation Army in his Ford truck, an ancient thing he'd driven forever. We walked into the small office, and a plump lady of about fifty sat me down in front of a desk. She had a name tag that read Sergeant Reed.

"Well, I must say this is highly unusual for such a young person to sign up." She opened a drawer and pulled out some forms for me to sign. "How did you come to want to be a bell ringer?"

Well, that was just the part I dreaded. "M-my g-g-grandma was a b-b-b-bell r-r-r-r-r-ringer." Oh, why couldn't I say the words right. Sometimes I hated my mouth. I could feel my face turning hot as I looked down at my feet.

"Why, that's lovely. Another generation. My!" She clapped her hands and I looked up. I guess my funny talking wouldn't keep me from doing my job. She handed me a bell and motioned for another worker to put the kettle on the back of Opa's truck. He hiked it up onto his shoulders, and we headed out the door.

I closed my eyes and said a little prayer, thankful I passed the bell ringer test. I watched the scattering flakes of snow streak past my window. The old truck shifted into third gear and heaved a groan as we chugged past the lake. I caught a glimpse of the amber rays dipping into Lake Michigan before disappearing into the horizon, signaling another day gone.

# —Chapter Ten—

## Help!

Coming home from the candy store, I heard a shriek from one of the manholes across the street from Oma and Opa's apartment. Now I know weird and strange things happen only in the movies, so I kept walking, thinking I was imagining something. About three yards past the drain on Eighth Street, I heard it again. It sounded way down under the pavement. Could it be a sewer rat? No, rats don't scream. Maybe it was a homeless person who decided to find an out-of-the-way place to spend the upcoming winter? I walked down the next block, but then I turned back, more from curiosity than any thoughts of rescuing any creatures. How scary could it be?

"Help!" the cry grew louder and more frantic. "Someone, help." I leaned over and tried to peer through the grates. It sounded like a person …

"Please," another plea, even fainter, drifted through the dark black slats. It sounded so pathetic.

I squatted down on the curb and cupped my hands together. "Hello?"

"I'm trapped down here," said the voice.

"Do you need help?"

There was a silence and then, "Duh. I said I'm trapped. Someone needs to get me out."

*Now what was I supposed to do?* I looked around, but I didn't see a grown- up anywhere on the street. I tried to pick up the grate, but it weighed a zillion pounds. "Sorry, it's too heavy."

"I'm going to die if you don't get help."

Well, that did it. I didn't want to go to heaven thinking someone kicked the bucket because I didn't rescue them. "Hold on. Wait there, and I'll be back."

I heard a faint snort. "Where do you think I'll go?"

*Geez, for someone in trouble he was certainly rude.* I dashed upstairs to my grandparents' apartment. "Someone's trapped underground and is dying."

"What?" said Oma. She didn't look like she believed me.

"It's true."

"I'll go with you to the police station. It'll be faster than calling. Let me grab my sweater." She rummaged around the coat closet in the hallway.

We rushed into the station and stood in front of the reception window. A man with sunken cheeks smiled at me. "So, what seems to be the problem, young lady?"

"My granddaughter thinks there's someone stuck underground right by our apartment on Eighth Street. She heard a voice."

"Does she usually hear voices?" said the sergeant, whose badge read Kenneth Vanderploeg. He didn't do a very good job of hiding his laughter.

"Now listen to me, young man. Someone's in trouble. Are you going to help or not?"

The bald man with sunken cheeks jerked to attention. "Yes, ma'am." He took down our names and phone number and the location of the manhole.

Five minutes later, we were standing in front of it.

"I'm still here. Can you get help?" The voice sounded thinner and full of fear.

"They're coming," I said.

The town's public works truck pulled up. "I understand you've been hearing sounds from the manhole," said a short burly man wearing a blue-and-yellow Michigan hat. I nodded and pointed to it. The city worker went around to the back of his truck and pulled out a long, metal rod with a hook on the end. He walked back to the hole and inserted a key into one of the smaller holes on the edge. With one push, he heaved the edge of the lid up. It flipped over and thundered onto the street. Oma and I jumped at least a foot off the ground.

"Heavy, eh?" The worker grinned and grabbed a high-beam flashlight  from his jacket pocket before climbing down a ladder on the side of the hole. I leaned over as his head became smaller. It looked like he was headed into a black lagoon.

"Hey, whatcha doin' down here, kid?" The worker's voice echoed down the bottom of the hole. "There's barely room for both of us." I didn't hear much of an answer, only a small whimper. "It's okay, I've got you," we heard the man reassure the kid. "Here, hang onto the side of the ladder and climb up. I'll be behind you." We heard some scuffling and then some steps on the ladder. A head appeared. I couldn't believe it. It was Noah from school. His eyes were swollen, and his face looked like a cream puff, only redder. I almost didn't recognize him.

"You can thank this little girl for hearing your shouts. She and her grandma went to the police department, and they notified Public Works about your situation."

"Thank you." Noah dropped his head.

I couldn't believe what had come out of his mouth. I guess God still preforms miracles.

"How the heck did you get down there? Surely you didn't open the lid off one of these monsters?" said the Public Works guy.

"I, I started exploring in that open drainpipe at Cedarwood Elementary with my buddy. We walked and walked to see where it would go. Then he got scared and went back the other way towards the school." Noah's teeth were chattering as he pushed out the words. "Can I sit down?"

"Sure." The city worker scratched his head. "It's at least two miles from that school to downtown. That could have been dangerous if a big rainstorm hit, which has been predicted for today. You'd have become bait for all the snakehead fish. You know, those Frankenfish that some yo-yo introduced into one of the creeks a few years ago." He clapped his palms together to imitate a fish's mouth.

Noah finally looked over at me, the color draining from his face, which made his freckles more noticeable. He looked like he'd viewed the creepy movie *Halloween* three times. "Thanks, Cassie. I'd still be down there if you hadn't heard me."

# —Chapter Eleven—

## *Mom's Home!*

"Mom!" I rushed into the apartment, and before I could stop, I slammed my whole body into hers. "I missed you." I wrapped my arms around her torso and leaned into her soft body, smelling her favorite perfume. Now Thanksgiving would be perfect.

"Well, that's quite a greeting. I missed you too. And the good news is that I won't have to work for a few days."

Opa walked into the room. "Yes, your mom just got here. We weren't expecting her until Friday."

"I know, last-minute change of plans." Mom sat down on the couch, kicked off her high heels, and plopped her bare feet on the coffee table. "Hope you have enough turkey for me."

"Glad you could make it for Thanksgiving, but a phone call would have been nice. Have you forgotten our number?" Oma put her hands on her hips.

"I got busy with an important account and then hit a big storm in the Upper Peninsula. Come on, Mom, I've been working my butt off. You know Christmas is coming."

"You have a daughter who misses you."

"And I miss her." Mom turned and tweaked my bangs. "Honey, got something for you." She leaned over the side of the sofa and pulled a bag out of her purse. She stood. "Come here, cutie."

I bounced over to her and took the bag. Inside was a shiny gold necklace with three of my birthstones, ruby. "Oh wow!" I let my fingers slide over the smooth rocks.

"Pretty impractical. Have you considered the kid needs new winter boots? We've had to make do with her ones from last year," said Oma.

"Oh hush, Edna," said Opa.

"For crap's sake, why didn't you tell me? I told you I'd send money if she needed something." My mother's disposition sank faster than a leaky rowboat. But just as quickly, she recovered as she took both my hands in hers. "Tomorrow we'll go shopping and pick up a nice pair at Kohl's. How's that sound?" She picked up her suitcase. "Here, help me carry my briefcase, Cassie." She headed back to our bedroom.

I followed her, relieved that I'd made my bed that morning and picked up some of my dirty clothes. Mom was very tidy, and I knew she'd be after me if my room was a mess. I dropped her briefcase onto the chair that separated the two beds, and she closed the door.

"I love my necklace, Mom."

"Cassie, my little ladybug. How I've missed you. We need to have some time together." She pulled the tie from her hair and shook her head "Are you doing okay in school?"

I plopped down next to her on the bed covered with a dark-green bedspread. The color reminded me of the Amazon forest, or at least what I imagined the jungle to look like, a place I'd like to visit someday.

"Yeah, I g-g-guess. I'm real good f-f-f-friends now with M-M-Marie Louise."

"That's nice." She stood, unzipped her suitcase, took out her

cosmetic bag, and put it next to her briefcase. "You always make friends."

I couldn't believe my ears. I had always had a hard time making friends, and Mom knew it. It took me a long time to make friends in Fayetteville. Had she already forgotten I talk funny, and no one likes a stammerer? It was like she lived in a different world from the rest of us. Maybe she liked her own made-up world better.

"Let's have you try on the necklace. It's genuine 14 karat gold, so take care of it."

I looked in the mirror. I had never seen anything so beautiful. It was a lot better than a dumb pair of winter boots, anyway. I smiled to myself. The necklace made me look more grown up. Wow, my first piece of real jewelry.

"Thanks, Mom, I love it."

"My pleasure."

"H-h-have you heard from D-d-dad lately? He's been sending me letters, but he hasn't called me."

Mom let out a long sigh. "You remember why. He injured his vocal cords in the explosion and has difficulty talking. It's going to take months before he can talk right again." She got that faraway look in her eyes, and it made me sad. "There are a lot of things that will have to be healed besides your father's injuries." She jumped up. "Enough of that. Your father is in a good hospital and in a few months will be transferred to Grand Rapids Mary Free Bed. Then we'll throw a big party for him!"

I slipped into my bed that night, planning the perfect party I'd have for Poppi when he came home. I'd make his favorite carrot cake, and we'd ask everyone we knew to celebrate. Now that would be a golden moment! Before I nodded off to sleep, I did what Poppi taught me to do at night. I counted on my ten fingers all my blessings. Let's see: Mom coming home, a new necklace, Poppi getting better, a good friend at school, Oma, Opa, hopefully some new winter boots, my favorite rice pudding for dinner, a warm house, and best of all, being a bell ringer.

The only thing that bothered me was why had Mom bought me such a nice necklace, and right before Christmas. She didn't usually give me expensive presents. Sometimes she would give me little unexpected gifts, but then forget my birthday. *I can't figure out Mom.*

I yawned and slid down deep into my covers. I had big plans for making money with the Red Kettle. All that night I dreamed of millions of children ringing bells as coins and dollar bills fell from the sky. I had collected so much money, it spilled out of the yellow plastic bucket Oma uses to put weeds in when she gardens the patch behind our apartment building.

# —Chapter Twelve—

*It's Official*

The Saturday after Thanksgiving, Opa knocked on my bedroom door. He came in and dropped an envelope onto my bed. "Got something for you."

The return address had a red kettle and a big red S. My hands shook a little as I opened the letter, which reminded me that I had to ring the bell and "To be sure to thank those that donate and keep a smile on your face. We are helping members of the community. Some of your donations received will be used to purchase gift baskets for the poor in our town."

I looked at Opa. His face beamed. "Ladybug, looks like you are following a family tradition. Well, get dressed for the snow, and we'll set up outside our apartment."

I watched him shuffle back to the living room, his shoulders draped over the walker's handles. He had grown older and slower in the last few years. I stuffed my feet into my new fur-lined boots, slipped into my parka, and followed my grandfather into the elevator that led outside to the sidewalk.

We dragged the kettle from the outside closet, and Opa steadied its legs. He stood with me as a mom and two little boys walked by. They smiled but didn't stop. A robust old man huddled against the winter wind, ignoring my bell ringing. Finally, a young boy in a camouflage jacket dropped a couple of quarters into the kettle.

"Your first donation!" My grandfather gave me a thumbs-up.

We stood as the afternoon snow accumulated, about two inches, and I could tell Grandpa was getting tired. "This cold is getting to my arthritis. My knees aren't the same as they used to be."

"I'll be okay. Can I stay out here a few more minutes?"

"Well ..."

"I'm doing fine. Go take your nap."

He peered down at me through his dark-rimmed glasses. "Sure you'll be okay? Well, I'll tell you what. I'll sit in the armchair by the front window upstairs and watch you. If anything happens and you need help, here's my phone. Only stay ten more minutes. It's almost dark." He headed toward the alley and stopped in front of the elevator. I watched him push the "Up" arrow before he disappeared into the side of the building.

I turned back to the sidewalk when I saw a familiar face bursting out of the thickening cloud of snowflakes. Noah. Why was he on my street? I pulled down my toboggan hat and turned toward the street, hoping he wouldn't recognize me. But he did.

"You think you're going to get money standing out here with that dumb bell?" he said. "Hey, that's your new name, Dumbbell." He scrunched up his face, stuck out his tongue, and disappeared into Mrs. H.'s store. A minute later she thrust open the door and stood in the doorway, her dark hair collecting bits of snow like a magnet.

"What's that racket? Child, you are driving me crazy with this ringing." She grabbed my hand. I looked into her large bug-out eyes, eyes that if not properly attached would easily spring out of their sockets. Why would she be so upset with my project? I didn't answer her as my mouth felt glued shut, and it wasn't because of the cold. My lips formed the beginning of a word, but it stuck in my throat. I coughed trying to free it, but it still stayed lodged inside of me. I closed my eyes tight, hoping she'd go back into her store and leave me alone.

But she stepped closer to me. "Listen, please quit ringing that bell before my customers leave. I'm having a very important open house for my best clients, and I can't think straight." She turned on her heel, jerked open the door, and thrust herself through the small doorframe.

In spite of my frozen cheeks, I felt tears warming them up. They dripped down into my neck and moistened my muffler. I was one soggy mess. All I wanted to do was my class project. I decided to go dry off in our apartment. I yanked open the door to the elevator, only to find myself slipping on a patch of ice in front of the threshold. Splat. I landed on my bottom. I knew it was going to hurt a lot tomorrow. I picked myself up and raced up the outside stairs.

"Well, that was fast." Oma, lounging in her recliner, looked up from her game show.

"I hate her."

"Now what happened?"

"Mrs. Huizenga yelled at me. She said I was ruining her open house and her sales. And you know what? Her face turns purple the louder she yells."

Opa laughed. "Purple? Really?"

"It was."

"Well, why don't you take a short break? There's some instant hot chocolate on the counter." Oma pointed to the kitchen.

Ten minutes later I trudged down to the elevator again. As the motor hummed, I thought how I wasn't going to let this lady ruin my project. I smiled to myself. I'd show her. I'd ring my bell as loud as I could. I picked up the cold piece of metal and shook it until I thought my arm would fly off. Then, taking a break, I peeked into the kettle.

*Oh no!* The few dollars and coins dropped by kind passersby had disappeared. I had forgotten to lock the kettle. I should never have left the money alone, even for a few minutes. I wondered how much was missing. Tears brimmed in my eyes, and I blinked, knowing they'd become icy streams flowing down my cheeks if I let them escape. *What should I do?* I closed my eyes as the fluffy flakes stung my nose.

I opened my eyes and saw Fifth Third Bank right across the street from me, as if someone had snapped their fingers with an answer, just like in the movies. I'd go into my bank account and take out some of my money to replace what was stolen. Poppi said you need to make right something that's been wrong. I shoved the kettle into the inside of the elevator and pushed the second-floor button.

In the apartment, my grandparents were busy watching the afternoon news, their backs facing the door. I slipped into my bedroom and opened my top dresser drawer. Under my underwear I found my savings passbook. I hid the passbook under my coat, sneaking past the backs of my grandparents' recliners. But I wasn't fast enough.

"Isn't it about time to come in?" asked Oma, still glued to the television.

"Uh-huh." I scooted by them, out the entrance and into the elevator. Once on the ground, I crossed the street and pushed open the glass door marked "Entrance" to my bank. I clenched my fists together and walked up to one of the windows, one of the few times I'd ever done banking alone, without my dad.

"How much do you want to withdraw, Cassie?" The tall brunette teller with the long nose leaned her head towards me. "You don't have a lot in your account."

I thought about how much money must have been stolen. I really didn't have any idea how much was missing. "Well, maybe $25.00."

She tapped some keys on her adding machine. "That will only leave you with $34.01." She opened her drawer and pulled out several bills and put them in a small envelope before handing it to me.

"Well, look who's here."

I turned my head around. It was Mrs. H. standing behind me. "Banking your proceeds for the day?"

"Uh, no. They collect it."

"I would hope not. No sense mingling your money with your donations. I only hope you are careful with your contributions." She put her hand on my shoulder, but it didn't seem like a friendly hand. It felt more like a warning. I did not like that lady and wondered what was wrong with her.

# —Chapter Thirteen—

## Best Friends

"Am I wearing the right clothes for being a bell ringer?" Marie Louise twirled around in her red quilted parka. The hood, trimmed in white fur, made my friend look like one of Santa's helpers. "Mom bought it especially for me."

"You look c-c-c-cooool." I handed her the bell and she went to work, ringing it. We huddled together against the cold. Marie Louise was the best gift I'd had since moving to New Netherlands. We watched a stream of people snake by on the late Friday afternoon and only a couple of them noticed us. One older grandmother did slip a couple of dollars into the slot and smiled at us. But other than that, we weren't doing too well.

"What will the money go for?" asked Marie Louise.

"I'm not sure. Maybe some of the poor people who live on Greenly Street. Or sometimes the Army donates to a needy family who has medical problems."

"How's Mrs. H.? Have you seen her today? You know she's Noah's mom."

I took Marie Louise's bell-ringing hand and stopped it midair. "What?"

She looked at me like, *don't you know anything*. "Oh, everyone knows about him. That why he's so mean."

"Well, I don't, so you'll just have to t-t-t-t-tell me, Marie Louise. Don't act like such a know-it-all." Marie Louise was one of those friends you could get mad at, and it wouldn't matter. We'd already had three fights at lunch and made up after school. Two were about boys we had crushes on, and one was about whether or not there was a prehistoric monster in the bottom of Lake Michigan. She really believed it, and I told her I thought she was dumb.

"Well, she's got leukemia. It's kind of slow-growing."

I put my hand to my mouth. "You mean, like cancer?"

"Yep, she found out a couple of years ago. She was never real nice and getting sick just made things worse. They say she only has a couple of years."

I gulped. No wonder she was so grumpy. "So why doesn't Noah live with her?"

"He does. One year he lives with her and the next with his dad, 'cause they're divorced. This is the year he lives with his dad, but he comes to help his mom with the shop. Only reason I know is he was in my second-grade class and was real upset."

"That doesn't m-m-mean he has to BE A LOSER." I said it so loud that a mom with her head down, pushing a stroller, jerked up in surprise. "Sorry," I said and smiled at her as she sped by.

"Yeah, he was a cool dude in first grade. Even gave me an 'I love you' valentine." She made a heart with her two hands and giggled. "Yuck."

"I would rip it up in front of his eyes if he ever dared to give me one. Or maybe sneak my mother's cigarette lighter to school and burn it at recess." An elderly gentleman and his wife stopped to drop a couple of dollars in the kettle.

"Th-th-thank you." I stopped ringing the bell for a moment.

"You two need to be singing Christmas carols." The wife, a tiny lady in a black plaid coat, nodded at me. The heat from my embarrassment could have melted the nearest snowdrift. I looked down at the ground then up at the cheerful face. "I c-c-can't talk, or s-s-sing."

"Oh, sure you can. Give it a try. We need more Christmas music. I'm a retired choir director, and I miss the old songs." I looked away. I didn't know what to say. Was she deaf? The last thing I'd do is sing in public. I could ring a bell but that's it. Final. No way was I going to sing on a public sidewalk.

The couple shuffled by. "That was weird," said Marie Louise.

"Yeah, some grown-ups don't get it."

"What?"

"You know, *some* of us have problems, Marie Louise. Like stuttering."

"Your only problem is Noah. Other than that, you're good. Except your father. And he's so brave."

"Yes."

"Like you."

# —Chapter Fourteen—

## *Trouble*

All eyes turned towards the black squad car that pulled up outside the front of the school at ten o'clock Thursday. One of the best things about being in the fifth grade was that all the classrooms had big windows that looked out onto the front parking lot. Usually there wasn't much to see, but having a cop car show up proved a great excuse for delaying the Social Studies test.

"Must be Miss Hathaway had too many overdue library books," Noah quipped. His friend Sam, fist-bumped him before smoothing out the wave in his hair. He knew the girls loved his hair.

Miss Hathaway walked over to the window to see what the class was looking at. "Pretty funny, Noah. I do tend to forget to return them. I guess you'll know Monday when you have a substitute teacher." She turned and watched a balding officer head through the front door. "All right, everyone, get ready for the test. It's not open book today."

Not more than ten minutes later Miss Hathaway answered the phone on her desk. Her face darkened as she looked up. "Cassie." She motioned for me to come.

I walked to the front of the room. In a low voice she said, "You need to go to the office." I noticed her eyes had a shadowed look, her mouth set in a grim line, but she patted me on the shoulder.

In the school office, I saw the policeman we'd spied outside. Next to him were my Oma and Opa.

"Sit down, honey," said Oma. She patted the seat of a wooden chair.

"We are sorry to have to talk to you, but something's come up with your mother," said the officer. He had a sad look in his narrow, brown eyes, like he didn't want to deliver his message. "Did you used to live at 340 East Eighth Street?"

I could hardly understand his words. It was like he was talking gibberish to me, and my mind wouldn't translate. Something told me I knew what this was going to be about. Finally, I squeaked out a "Yes."

"Was the condo furnished when you moved in?"

"Y-Y-Y-Yes."

"Did you and your mother bring any furniture up from Fayetteville?"

"No, just c-c-clothes and s-s-stuff."

He paced back and forth in front of the three chairs in the principal's office, like he had something important to decide. Was Mom in trouble? Why did he ask about the furniture? I looked at my grandparents, and they looked scared. Oma grabbed my hand and gave it a hard squeeze.

"I'd like to continue this discussion. Can you make it to the police station by 2:00 this afternoon?" the officer asked them. They nodded. He left, and we were all alone in the room.

Finally, Oma spoke up. "Honey, they've arrested your mother. She sold the furniture in the apartment where you'd been staying."

I put my hands over my ears and dropped my head onto the table. My whole body shivered with the news. I didn't want to hear this. And just when I was getting a good start in the town. But where was Mom? Did he say arrested? "Does that mean she's in jail?"

"Afraid so," said Oma, shaking her head. "Will that girl of ours ever get some sense into her?"

"Your mother put all the furniture on Craig's List and ..." said Oma.

"She sold it," said Opa.

"The place is completely empty. She's been making deals left and right with people. They carted away a sofa, two beds, a kitchen table, and chrome stools. They came from Fenville, Grand Haven, and Byron Center."

I remembered those stools. I loved those stools. *Oh, Mom, how could you?*

The ride home took five minutes, but it seemed like an hour as I listened to my grandparents talk quietly in the front seat of their old Ford Explorer.

"She says it's a big misunderstanding. By George, we didn't raise her to do those kinds of things." Opa slapped his hand on his knee in disgust.

Oma turned to Opa, her voice growing shriller. "We told her we'd help her as much as we could, but no, she's too stubborn to ask for help."

"Well, she's our daughter. We can't abandon her, and she has been through a lot," said Opa.

"Shh." Oma lowered her voice. "We'd never abandon her. But it's Cassie I hurt for. I hope this doesn't get out." She dabbed her eyes with a wadded-up tissue, and when she turned her head, I saw their rims had grown red.

"You know it will. Jillian looks for the easy way out. Just glad we have Cassie. Poor little kid."

I was mad at Mom. And I didn't want to be anyone's "poor Cassie." This wasn't a golden moment. It was a tarnished, miserable moment. Dad was wrong, I wasn't going to find any golden moments, at least not in this town.

# —Chapter Fifteen—

## Class Spy

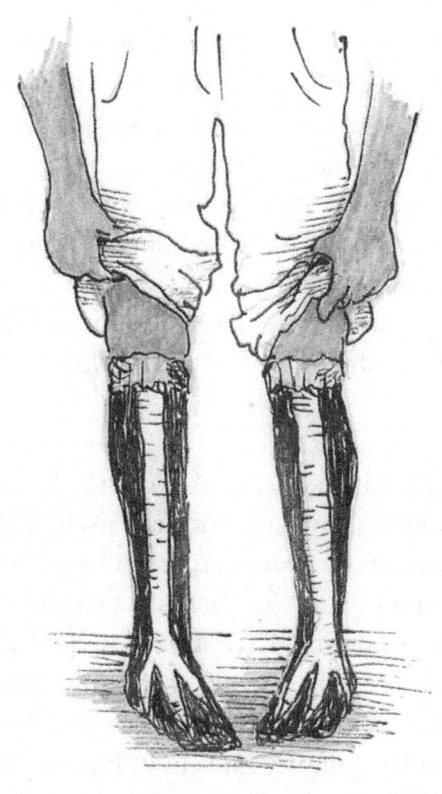

The next morning, Marie Louise stopped by my desk and whispered in my ear, "Meet me in the bathroom." She put her fingers to her lips, not wanting Miss Hathaway to hear.

Our teacher had already given the class a big lecture on girls meeting two and two in the restroom to work out personal issues. "Problems don't need to be worked out during class time."

Marie Louise left with the wooden bathroom pass, and I had to wait five minutes until Angela Vanderkliest got back. She liked to go to the bathroom during math class because she hated math. Everyone knew that but Miss Hathaway.

I trotted down the hallway, my boots making a clacking sound against the cement floor. I pushed open the restroom's heavy wooden door. Marie Louise was washing her hands, and when she saw me in the mirror she turned around. "I know about your mom."

"Oh."

"Oh, nothing. It's okay. I've already talked to a couple of kids at the bus stop, and I said I'd bust their rear and bring my four brothers to help if they said anything to you." She held up a closed fist.

I had to laugh. Marie Louise looked ridiculous. She was such a tiny girl, and her petite hand was the size of one of those green apples that hadn't even ripened in the fall, the kind boys like to pitch at you during class field trips to an orchard. She, like me, had to buy all her clothes in the little girl's department, but her size never stopped her. She wasn't afraid to take on anyone.

"R-R-R-Really?"

"Of course, dork. Ain't nobody gonna hurt my friend."

"Your mom probably won't want me to come over."

"Are you kidding? She loves you. You eat everything she bakes, even the weird stuff, like licorice cake and banana cheddar muffins. When you come over, I don't have to eat that junk."

I started to cry. "I'm so scared for my mom. She's really done it this time."

"Well, anyway, she's not you." She scrunched up the hem of her jeans and pulled them up to her knees. "Hey, this will make you laugh. Look what I'm wearing, ostrich leg socks." I glanced down at the front of her black knee-high socks. Two skinny gray ostrich legs ran down the front of the socks, attached to ostrich feet. "If you look at my socks, it looks like I have ostrich feet. Here, watch them dance." She moved her legs back and forth. "Thought you needed something funny today."

I giggled. "Cool. Thanks."

She let her pant legs drop just as Jessimyn busted in. That girl had a way of knowing just when to show up and butt in. Her smirk told me she knew something was up. "Miss Hathaway said you guys weren't supposed to be in here so long and told me to get you."

"Or did you volunteer to come spy on us?"

"You're such a brat, Marie Louise." Jessimyn turned to me. "She's pretty mad."

"O-k-k-kay, Miss P-P-Perfect, guess we'll have to stop t-t-talking about you."

She scrunched up her nose, which made her spiteful eyes look like two slits. She looked like a little piglet. "I'm telling."

"Tell and you'll never get to see my ostrich feet."

"You're not supposed to bring dead animal parts to school."

"Guess Marie Louise w-w-will have to t-t-take it out of your desk before it s-s-s-starts to smell."

Marie Louise and I held our stomachs, watching her eyes flit back and forth to see if we were kidding.

"Go check," I said.

"You guys are in so much trouble."

"I love trouble," said Marie Louise.

# —Chapter Sixteen—

## No Singing

After school the next day, I was in my room playing Zelda on the computer when Oma knocked.

"I talked to your teacher, and she said she'd support your project as long as you keep out of Mrs. H.'s hair and not block traffic."

"I never b-b-blocked…"

"And …"

"And what?"

"You're not to sing any Christmas carols. That would make it a religious project."

I sighed, the breath slowly leaking from my lips. "I'd never sing in public. I hate people looking at me. It's hard enough ringing a bell."

She sat down next to me on the bed and squeezed my hand. "I know it's hard for you to be in front of people, sweetie. All the more reason I'm glad you are following in our footsteps."

"I wanted to make you proud, especially since Mom let you down." I wanted to put back the twinkle in her eye, the one she lost when she found out about Mom.

"You do make me proud, every day. You were a brave girl to come up here with only your mom and start a new school." She pulled me closer so I could snuggle up to her, her itchy wool cardigan scratching my cheek.

"I'm tired of being brave and being brave alone."

"Sometimes we are called to be brave alone. Anyway, you have me and Opa."

"I know, but you can't be at school with me like a brother or sister."

"Siblings are a mixed bag. I grew up in a big family with six kids. Oh my, it was so noisy, and someone was always fighting or whining. What I remember was wanting to be alone sometimes. Anyway, God gave you Marie Louise. Even if you don't look anything like each other, you have a friend who is closer than a sister. Be thankful for what you do have."

After school the next day, I saw familiar handwriting scribbled on an envelope propped up against a glass vase on the table in the hall. Poppi! I tore open the letter with my finger, the envelope fluttering to the ground. I raced to my room, flung myself onto the bed, and unfolded it. It read:

Dear Ladybug,

You know I call you that because the ladybug is the cutest bug, just like you. I miss you terribly, but because I can't talk due to my throat, we'll have to send letters the old-fashioned way and post photos on Instagram.

I'm so happy you have a friend, Marie Louise. She sounds like a loyal friend and lots of fun. You don't need a lot of friends in life, only a few good ones. Sounds like your class project is taking off. Keep ringing that bell and you will raise a lot of money. So proud of how you've done. And don't worry about the stuttering. I do think it will get better. Anyway, most people talk too much. You've learned how to be a good listener.

I have a couple of buddies here, Jason and Rob. They're both from North Carolina. They're good guys, but it's not the same as family. If I've taught you anything, it's that you should treasure your family. Family might not look like you think it should.

I'm sure you miss North Carolina, but just think, you're seeing a lot of snow for the first time. Enough to sled in and make snowmen. I'm jealous!

Love you so much,<br>Poppi

I took the letter and put it under my pillow. I'd sleep better knowing it was there. Sometimes when I woke up in the middle of the night, scared about Mom, or lonely for Poppi, I would reread his letters. It was almost like he was talking to me. Except that he couldn't talk at all until his throat healed. I guessed stuttering wasn't so bad, at least I could say stuff. *I'm lucky to have such a brave father*, I said to myself.

Someone knocked on my door. "Come in," I said.

"Good letter?" Oma asked, standing at the doorway, wearing her favorite yellow-flowered apron but with a melancholy expression on her face. I was sure Mom had put it there.

"Dad's the best writer ever."

"I know! Your mom says he's probably going to be able to come home in the spring."

"You talked to her?"

"Yes, this afternoon." Her voice dropped. "She wants to see you, sweetie. We're going after supper tonight."

"I don't want to go."

Opa appeared behind Oma. "Now, sweetie, she's your mom."

"She's embarrassed m-m-me." I crossed my arms. I didn't want to see her for a long time. What a stupid thing to do. Couldn't she have worked harder at her job instead of stealing furniture? Or did she need money for something else?

"We understand. But holding a grudge isn't helping anyone."

"I have too much math homework tonight. I want to keep my grades up."

Oma sighed. "Your grades are outstanding. You could work really hard and finish it before supper."

"No, I can't."

"Suit yourself," said Opa and turned his walker around to head back to the living room. Oma shook her head at me and followed him.

Dinner that night was quiet with neither of my grandparents saying much. "I'll do the dishes, Oma," I said as they headed out the door.

"Sure you don't want to come?" my grandfather asked.

"Yes." I had a knot in the pit of my stomach that grew larger by the minute. I could feel it pull across my belly button, stretching until it might snap like a rubber band. Opa shrugged.

# —Chapter Seventeen—

## Field Trip

I hated the smell of diesel fuel. It reminded me of the time Mom and I had to take a Greyhound bus from Fayetteville to Charlotte to visit my dad's aunt, who was dying. I can still hear the bus gears changing from first to second as we bounced along the road, returning home after we had visited her in the nursing home. Funny how smells remind you of memories, some not so good. I stood in line at school, waiting to board the bus for the Gerald R. Ford Presidential Museum field trip to Grand Rapids while holding back a woozy stomach.

"Listen up, students," said Miss Hathaway doing our class's routine of clapping and responding. She clapped a rhythm and we clapped it back. Her system worked a lot better than yelling at us to "Shape up and quiet down." She wore a coat made of white fake fur and looked like a large fluffy rabbit. Her leather gloves gripped a clipboard. "I am assigning everyone a seat to mix things up. You will not be able to choose your seat partner. Today's trip will encourage you to get to know some of the students in our class you don't know well."

She looked like she thought that was a genius idea.

I scanned the crowd. No one else thought it was such a great idea. Standing in line to board, Marie Louise and I exchanged looks. We had made plans all week to sit together, trade candy and snacks, and snicker about the stupid boys in class. Now Miss

Hathaway had to go and ruin our plans. Didn't she know half the reason for a big bus ride is to spend time with your bestie?

She read out loud the seat partners as kids groaned and filed into the bus. The last two names were mine and Noah's. I now wondered if Miss Hathaway liked me. I would rather have stood on top of the school roof in my underwear and sang the Star-Spangled Banner than sit with him. *What* was Miss Hathaway thinking?

Noah must have seen the look on my face because the first thing he said to me when he found his seat by the window was, "Hey, I'm not too excited either." He and I were in the far back seat where the diesel fumes congregated. I popped a mint to ease my queasy stomach and looked straight ahead. "Yeah, go ahead and be stuck up," said Noah.

I ignored him, my gaze fixed on the hydraulic handle up front that opened the bus door. I could do this, I could survive forty-five minutes looking out the window at the blustery landscape. Oma said sometimes we have to be brave alone, and I guessed that time had come.

We sat in silence until out of the corner of my eye I saw Noah pull something out of his back jeans pocket.

"Want some?" He offered me a stick of gum. I focused on his chin, not wanting to look at him directly. His chin had an indent, what Mom called a cleft. *Weird, I have the same kind.* I wasn't very excited that we shared *anything* in common.

"I guess so. Thanks." I took the stick of gum from his hand and unwrapped the outer paper and the inner wrapping and popped it into my mouth. I hoped it wasn't poisonous. His fingers gripped the metal back of the seat ahead, his nails bitten down to the quick, ugly and red. The backs of his hands were round and plump. That was the only plump part of his body as he was rather bony and tall. He looked straight ahead.

"W-w-we're supposed to f-f-fill out this questionnaire about getting to know your seatmate," I said as I unfolded the paper and smoothed it out. I pulled a pen out of my backpack.

He turned his head to me, his scowl telling me all I needed to know. Still, I continued.

"So where were you born?"

He sighed. "None of your business."

"We have to get this done for extra credit."

"In Australia."

"H-h-hey, me too." I could play his game.

"So."

"What is your favorite television show?"

"Let me guess yours. *The Voice*, cause you're such a good singer."

I shrugged and plowed through. "Where would you like to live when you're older?"

He lowered his head and sighed in resignation, his chin tipping down to his chest. "Okay, the South."

"Really?"

"But not North Carolina. I want to live on Hilton Head Island, South Carolina. I'm going to be a golf pro someday."

"Wow."

"Wow, what? I have dreams. Just because my parents want to live at the North Pole doesn't mean I have to."

"But New Netherlands is a nice town. I like it."

"You only got here. Just wait."

"W-w-well, at least you have a s-s-sister and brother. You're l-l-lucky, I always wanted a sibling."

He turned his head back to the aisle and rolled a rubber ball to his buddy Sam at the front of the bus. Sam caught it and rolled it back to him.

It looked like I wasn't going to get my extra credit after all. I filled in what I could and folded the slip of paper, sliding it into my backpack. Maybe he'd be in a better mood when we came back. I really wanted that extra credit.

# —Chapter Eighteen—

## *Emergency*

"Class, what a great day we had, right? Miss Hathaway stood at the front of the bus, and the class lined up to head back home. The bus engine rumbled as it prepared for the trip. A small murmur, mainly from the girls in the class, answered her. "All of you will sit in your assigned seats, the same ones you had when you rode over here. No switching."

There went our second plan. Marie Louise and I had planned to play the fortune cookie game with each other. She had folded a piece of paper into the shape of the cookie. The person holding the folded object would put their thumbs and pointy fingers inside the four openings and move the paper model back and forth, spelling out colors, numbers, and names. You could ask it your favorite color, how many kids you would have, and the first initial of who you'd marry.

Reluctantly, I headed to the back of the bus to find my seat next to my least favorite person. I took a look. *Yep, he still hates me.* His lower lip stuck out so far, a mouse could have used it as a diving board. I giggled at the thought as I kicked my backpack under the seat. The bus driver slammed the stick shift into first gear as he pulled out of the parking lot and onto the interstate.

"Hey, move over, you're hogging the seat. It's that big fat coat that takes up all the room," said Noah.

I glared at him but didn't budge. "It's a d-d-dividing line to keep us s-s-separate, so I won't have to get near you and smell your stinky boots."

"Whatever." We rode along in silence, the windows steaming with condensation and the tiny bus heater blaring out its meager warmth. After a few moments, the cold got to me, and I picked up my coat from the seat and wiggled my arms into it. I turned my head and noticed a funny look on Noah's face. The sneer was gone, and in its place, a strange expression. His mouth was open, but he wasn't saying anything. Then his eyes rolled back into their sockets, and his body twitched and convulsed as his limbs stiffened I knew exactly what was happening. I'd had a friend in North Carolina who had seizures and told me about them, but I'd never seen one for myself. I remembered one thing, though, to keep sharp objects away from the person.

I leaned over and grabbed a pencil that was sticking out of the backpack he was holding on his lap. If he had fallen over it would have poked him in the eye or skull or who knows where. Then I screamed for Miss Hathaway.

She flew back as two rows of heads followed her fuzzy white coat. I kept watching as his limbs began to spasm. "Oh, please don't die," I thought. "God, I'm sorry for all the mean things I thought about Noah."

The bus pulled over, and I let Miss Hathaway sit in my seat. Noah was coming out of it and opened his eyes. He gazed ahead like he was sleepwalking. Miss Hathaway took his hand and squeezed it. "You'll be all right, Noah. Just relax." She turned to the class.

"Everyone, mind their own business and finish filling out your homework sheet on President Gerald Ford. Get busy!" She clapped her hands to show she was serious and turned to me. "You can have my seat up front."

I handed her the pencil. "It was in his backpack and he almost fell on it. I know about this stuff because my friend in North Carolina had seizures."

"Good job, Cassie. You saved him from injuring himself. Now go get settled up front." She turned to Noah. "I've called your mom, and she will be here in about twenty minutes."

The next day at morning break, it was warm enough that we could all go outside if we put on boots, hats, and gloves. Miss Hathaway was very strict on that rule. She said she didn't want any frostbite on her watch. I didn't know what she was watching as the aides were the only ones who had to go outside for recess.

"Let's go," said Marie Louise, who dribbled a basketball. Even being quite short, she was still a good shot. It helped that she had four older brothers to practice with.

"I guess." But I changed my mind when I saw Noah standing near the backboard. "No, let's not." I grabbed the ball and tried to jerk her past a group of guys dribbling up and down the half court that had been shoveled off by the custodian. Too late.

Noah leaned against the pole. He cupped his hands like a megaphone. "Oh, there's my seatmate. Bet she gets extra credit for her good deed." He grinned at his friends.

"Hear she plans on being a doctor," said Sam.

Marie Louise turned to me. "No good deed goes unpunished, my mama always says. Of all the ungrateful, jerky, obnoxious people, he takes the cake." She squeezed her gloved hands together and rushed up to the court, where she shot the ball. It swished through the net. Dribbling it off the court, she let it drop to the ground before she punted it down to the other side of the playground. "For your information she did save you, jerk. You would have fallen into the pencil you were holding and put a big old hole in your forehead if she hadn't taken it away."

Noah's eyes widened. He stared at me and then announced it was too cold for b-ball.

"Snowball fort at the end of the yard." He and Sam waved their tribe of guys down to the far corner of the yard where the two corners of the cyclone fence met.

I caught her sleeve and pulled her to the side of the building. "Let's do inside recess, and we can play the f-f-fortune cookie game. Besides, I don't want you to end up in the principal's office. I've b-b-been there and it's gross. Smells like s-s-sour milk and throw-up from kids who puked while waiting for their parents to pick them up when they're s-s-sick." My sensitive nose sometimes made my life miserable.

"Okay," said Marie Louise as she pulled out the paper fortune cookie from her parka. "But I don't get why he treats you so bad. What did you ever do to him?"

"Be born?"

# —Chapter Nineteen—

## Counting Money

"So how much have you collected from the red kettle?" asked Marie Louise as she reached for another windmill-shaped cookie. "Wow, your grandma rocks at making cookies. When is she going to open a bakery?" She took a bite out of the spiced goody and wiped the crumbs off her mouth.

"I'll tell her you like them. She and Opa are visiting my mom."

"You're not going to see her?" Marie Louise tipped her head and scrunched up her face. "She's your mom."

"So?"

"So, she might want to see her only kid. She stole that furniture so she could get money for your dad's rehab."

"Yeah, r-r-right."

"You don't believe her?"

I picked up our two empty milk glasses, put them in the sink, and turned on the water to rinse them off. Oma was very particular about dirty dishes on the table. "Let's count my kettle money." I had missed the man who picks up the kettle, so I brought a sack of it into the apartment. I opened a cupboard above the stove, pulled out a plastic container full of coins with a few dollars, and popped off the top. Marie Louise and I split up the pile, counting to ourselves. I piled the one- and five-dollar bills in a pile and counted them.

"I have $8.00," said Marie Louise.

"Including the bills, I have $34.64. That's not much."

"Sure it is."

"No." I went to the refrigerator and pulled a sheet of paper out from underneath a magnet that said, "Great Lakes, Shark-Free Swimming."

"The money goes for feeding the poor, sending kids to camp, disaster relief, and re-h-h-ha, re-ha-bil-a-tation, whatever that is. How can $42.64 do all that? We've got to have more."

Marie Louise and I looked at the red poinsettia plastic tablecloth and the puny pile on the table. Lots of pennies and nickels but not many quarters. "Guess we need some help," she said.

"Might be a g-g-good time for it, God." I rolled my eyes upwards towards the ceiling. I needed a lot of miracles right now.

# —Chapter Twenty—

## Life's Not Fair

Oma and Opa came back in time for supper. "Sorry you didn't come with us," said Oma, staring down her nose at me as she set a large takeout bag on the table. "Thought we'd pick up some burgers from Burger Hut. Good night to not cook." She went to the cupboard and pulled out some paper plates, set them on the table, and put one foil-wrapped sandwich on each plate. Then she split up the large order of fries. I rooted around the fridge for ketchup, mayo, and mustard, a must for Opa's burger. I thought if I could keep busy setting the table, they wouldn't ask me a bunch of questions.

"No Marie Louise?" Opa looked around.

"Her mom came and picked her up."

We sat down and held hands. Opa cleared his throat. "Dear Lord, we thank you for the warmth of our home and your bountiful food. Keep us healthy and ever mindful of your blessings, especially family. Keep Jillian safe until she is released and let us walk in forgiveness, remembering we all have sinned. Amen."

Oma took a tiny bite of the edge of her bun and swallowed. "Your mother asked about you. She also insists the whole incident is a mistake."

My sweater, which was last year's and too small, felt tight like a large green snake was choking me. I dipped a French fry into a puddle of ketchup on my plate. "Oh," was all I could mutter.

"She misses you terribly."

"Then why did she do that stupid thing?" I swallowed and the fry lodged in my throat like it wanted to stay there permanently. I took a large gulp of milk.

Oma reached for my hand, her jingling charm bracelet dancing as light from the kitchen table's overhead lamp caught its sparkle. "The landlord may have not listened very well to your mother's plan to sell the furniture for him. That is a distinct possibility. Your mother does have some zany ideas at times."

Hot shame flared from my neck to the top of my head. Should I have visited her? My angry thoughts battled with my grandparents' kindness. But it wasn't fair what she did. It was wrong and on top of that, embarrassing. I knew kids talked behind my back at school. Didn't she care about that? How about my suffering?

Almost as if he had heard my thoughts, my Opa slammed down the ketchup bottle with a thud. He lowered his head. I looked away.

"Look at me," he said. I brought my eyes up to his, blinking back tears. "Life isn't fair. The sooner you learn that, the better. Some people have a lot of strikes against them and ..."

"Like me."

"No, your mother. Try to see her side."

"She doesn't have to sit on the bus and hear the snickering."

"Snickering is the least of our problems. Have a little compassion, young lady," said Opa.

I grabbed my elbows and squeezed. I was wearing a long sleeve sweater, but if I had seen the skin, I was sure they'd be purple by now.

"And stop squeezing your elbows, you'll cut off the circulation. Your mother has had your father severely injured in Afghanistan. He's recovering far away …"

"But."

"Shhh. She had to quit her job and move back to her hometown where she has bad memories. She's been traveling on the road and is about exhausted trying to get some money together for you to have a nice Christmas."

I didn't say anything. Somehow when Opa explained all our problems to me, it made more sense. Mom was suffering, too.

"I never thought about Mom that way."

"She has feelings, too." Oma added her bit of advice, and now I was really feeling crummy. "I know it seems like she did something terrible but try to be a bit understanding. Your mother cracked under a lot of pressure."

"Will she be in jail very long?"

"We hired a lawyer and are trying to get the charges dropped. The people who purchased the furniture have returned it, and your mother has emptied her bank account so that all but about

$100.00 has been repaid. I think she has a good case." Oma reached into the Burger Hut bag and pulled out a paper napkin. Gently, she dabbed my wet cheeks with it. "Now have another bite of hamburger before it goes cold. Those burgers weren't cheap, and we don't want to waste them."

Obediently, I bit into the sandwich. The melted cheese and broiled meat soothed my rumbling stomach. We ate the rest of the meal in silence.

I stood and gathered the trash and beverage glasses. "Can we have ice cream for dessert?"

"Sure, why not," said Opa.

"I have one question for you and Oma."

"Shoot."

"Why does my mom hate New Netherlands so much? What happened that made her leave? She always grumbles about being here."

My grandparents exchanged glances, but no one answered.

My stomach hurt all the next day at school, and I couldn't eat dinner that night. "*Eet smakelijk*, enjoy," said Oma as she placed bowls of mushy split pea soup on the plates in the dining room. I tried not to throw up inside of my mouth. It wasn't my favorite meal. She found her place at the table and grabbed my and my grandfather's hands. "So, we pray and thank the Lord for the good things."

I didn't feel very thankful for much. My mother was still in jail, my father was in the hospital, and the most popular boy in school hated me. On top of everything else, I was probably going to flunk the community service project. I guessed it wouldn't be so bad if I had a sibling I could talk to, or even better, a big brother who could tell stupid Noah off.

"Cassie? Do you want to add anything?" Opa had said thanks and was looking at me like it was my turn.

"Uh, thanks for my awesome grandparents, and my parents, and good split pea soup." I opened my eyes and both Oma and Opa were staring at me.

"You hate split pea soup," said Opa, shaking his head. He reached for my hand and cradled it, and I felt comfort in its warm, dry cocoon.

"She does?"

"You don't pay attention, Oma. I always notice she only eats a partial bowl when you serve it." He grinned at me. "Maybe we need to serve you some barbecued pork and hushpuppies?" He let out a raspy laugh, and I couldn't help but smile.

"That's better," he said. We ate in silence with the Jeopardy television program droning like background music. In their mid-seventies, both my grandparents believed that watching the quiz show would stave off Alzheimer's, so they watched it every night.

"History for fifty," said Oma, calling out to the television from the kitchen. "Okay, how was the day?" She put a bowl of bread pudding in front of me. "I know there is something troubling our girl."

I reached for the small pitcher of hot lemon sauce and poured it over the top. It made up for the yucky soup. "Well, one of the most popular boys in school hates me, and I miss Poppi."

"Noah?" said Opa. "Noah Huizenga?"

"Yeah, the one who had a seizure? He didn't even thank me for saving his life when he almost fell on a pencil before I grabbed it."

"Why do you think he doesn't like you?" said Opa, reaching for another spoonful of pudding. Oma clucked her tongue and pointed to his stomach as if to say, "Do you need seconds?"

I swallowed. "I don't know."

"Who wouldn't like this lovely specimen of a girl," said Opa as he wrapped his arm around my neck and gave me a peck on the cheek.

"Well, that's because you're my Opa. You have to say that."

"It's true. It's in the grandparent contract."

Oma clapped her hands together. "That reminds me, your father is going to do that Zoom thing with us tonight. Will that cheer you up?" She looked at the grandfather clock in the corner. "Heavens, it's almost time." She ran to the bedroom for the laptop, placed it on the kitchen table, and booted it up. Grabbing the mouse, she clicked on the link.

"There's Poppi!" I screamed at the top of my lungs when I saw the familiar face propped up by a pillow as he lay on his bed.

"How's my ladybug?"

"Are you okay?" I asked.

"They fitted me for my new legs today."

"Really?"

"Yep."

"Are you coming home soon?"

"We'll see. I've had a bronchial infection, so the doctors are watching me carefully. But enough about me. Where's your mom? Haven't heard from her for a week or two. I know she's probably busy being on the road."

I froze. Oma jumped in. "Hi there, stranger. Looking good. Jillian has been tied up, but she sends her love."

"Yeah, it's weird. I've been trying to contact her. Is her phone broken?"

I jumped in. "Poppi, you've got to come home. I miss you terribly." I hoped I didn't sound too desperate, but I was. He could fix this mess and talk to Mom.

"Trying to, ladybug."

I told him more about my friend Marie Louise and that I was getting good grades. I also told him everything I liked about the new town. I didn't tell him any of the bad things. He had enough problems right now. We signed off but not before he reminded me to look for the golden moments.

# —Chapter Twenty-One—

## *Burglars*

I waited in the Ottawa County jail's parking lot while Oma and Opa went inside to pick up Mom. I knew it took a lot of money for my grandparents to pay for a lawyer. They had to cash a savings bond at the bank. I hoped Mom appreciated what they did.

"Hello, ladybug." My mother tapped at the window, opened the door, and slid her bottom across the seat. She reached out and wrapped her arms around me. "Oh, how I missed you."

"Are you home for good?"

"Honey, the landlord dropped the charges. We misunderstood each other. I thought I'd help him by selling the furniture on Craig's List because he was putting the apartment up for sale anyway. He doesn't remember our conversation and thought I was stealing his stuff. But it's okay now."

Sometimes it amazed me how optimistic my mother could be when she got in trouble. She always thought there was a pot of gold at the end of each mishap. I probably worried enough for both of us.

"Can we drive through Starbucks? I haven't had a good cup of coffee for the last eight days."

"I suppose, but we do have coffee at home," said Oma. She hated spending any extra money on extravagant coffee drinks. Nevertheless, Opa turned left and drove the five blocks.

"My treat," said Mom.

"Save your money, Jillian," said Oma. I could tell she was getting mad at Mom by the set of her mouth and the way her right eyelid twitched. She probably didn't think there was anything so special about spending $17.89 to celebrate something that shouldn't be celebrated. We drove through the drive-through and headed back south on 131 with only the windshield wipers swishing away snow to break the silence.

After finishing her latte, Mom said, "Hate to tell you this, and you may have figured this out, but I can't go back to my apartment. Looks like I'll have to stay with you. I can stay in Cassie's bedroom like I have been if that's okay."

"Of course." Opa turned his head toward the back seat to glance at Mom, and the car swerved to the right. Sometimes I wonder about Opa. He didn't always pay attention when he was driving.

"Bob, you barely missed that ditch." Oma shook her head and looked heavenward, like she might be headed there any minute.

"Anyway … you are welcome to stay for a while. You are still our daughter, and we love you," said Opa, before glaring at Oma. They always squabbled about his driving. Oma said she hoped there weren't cars in heaven. She'd had enough bad driving with Opa on earth.

Mom patted his shoulder. "I'm so sorry about this. I don't know what I was thinking. And I need to move out of the lease by this weekend. Don't have much left there but a few boxes." She looked out the window. "Guess I'm always saying sorry to you.'"

"We will help. We always do," said Oma, drawing her brows together in one big frown as she watched the speedometer's hand slowly rise and pass the speed limit. Opa may walk slowly, but he made up for that slowness when he slipped behind the wheel.

"I have the best parents," said Mom.

"You sure do," said Oma.

That night, I lay in my bed looking out the window. Mom had the bed to the wall, and I had the window view, which I loved. Snoozy usually slept at the bottom of my bed but Oma had taken him to the vet that day because he was having breathing problems and he had to stay there overnight.

I had pulled back the curtain to look down on Eighth Street. I loved how the whole street was covered with Christmas lights. Lights on the streetlamps, lights in the window displays, lights on the trees, like an imaginary world that glistened in the snow. I listened to my mother's even breathing and stared out through the glass at the evening sky. On cold, cloudless nights I felt like I could touch the stars. It looked like someone had taken paint and spackled the black satin sky. So many of them. I wondered how long it took God to pitch them up into the heavens.

Did He do it every night? I hoped Dad could see them tonight. Summers in Fayetteville when he was home, he used to wake me up after Mom went to bed. Rumpled in my sleep clothes, I held his hand as he led me out to the porch. We'd sit quietly on our wooden swing, listening to the frogs sing their night lullaby, and if we were lucky, the hoot owl that lived in the trunk of the ancient poplar tree would greet us. I could still feel the humid air making my pj's stick to my skin as I brushed sweat off my forehead. My dad pointed out the constellations and slipped a moon pie into my awaiting hand. We had a contest seeing who could find the North Star first, but now that I was older and thinking back, I bet he'd let me win. He was like that. Maybe *that* was what he meant by a golden moment.

I looked over at Mom, who was in the depths of a dream. By the light of the full moon, I could see her lips curved up, her hair fanned out over the pillowcase. I'm sure she didn't sleep well. A wave of regret swept through my mind. I should have visited her in jail. *She's my mom, for the good and bad.* The good was when she was full of energy. She could clean the house in two hours, bake a dessert, and paint a bedroom with plenty of energy to spare. The bad happened when she slipped into her dark moods and stayed in her bathrobe all day. Those days I cooked dinner and made excuses for her being sick when her boss called. I'd become pretty good at making baked potatoes, fish sticks, and brownies.

*Bam.* I froze. Someone was on the outside staircase that ran next to the elevator in the alley. I listened as the side of the house shook with footsteps climbing higher and higher. Who was that? No, it was more than one person. I heard at least two voices whispering. "Head for the balcony off of the living room. And don't drop it."

Drop what? A gun? A baseball bat that could break the front window? Burglars weren't common, and anyway we didn't have anything valuable except Opa's computer, his gold watch he got when he retired from Hayworth, and Oma's pearl-and-silver necklace. But how would thieves know about them?

Not being a very brave person, I snatched my pillow and crawled under my bed. My heart thudded faster than when my teacher gave us the Presidential Youth Fitness Test in North Carolina, and I thought it might explode. My poor mom and grandparents would find my limp, dead body in the morning.

# —Chapter Twenty-Two—

## *Mom Heads to School*

"Wake up. For heaven's sakes, why are you under that bed?" My mother shook my arm and proceeded to drag me out from under the bed frame.

I stood and rubbed my eyes. "I didn't want the robbers to kill me."

"Any robbers that come to this house won't find much to pilfer. Now get your clothes on before you miss the bus. It's too cold to walk today."

"Did they get anything?"

"Who?"

"The burglars."

"I swear, you are the biggest worrywart kid I know." She walked to my chest of drawers and pulled out my undies, socks, a thick red sweater, and some jeans.

The doorbell rang. It was our neighbor, Mr. Jacob. He shook the powdered snow off his parka. "Have you not seen the banner hanging off of the balcony?" He hobbled over to the front patio door that overlooked the street, and Oma pulled open the drapes. A paper banner was fastened to the railing, attached with duct tape. It was about six feet wide.

"What on earth?" She walked outside and looked over the railing, before letting out a shriek. "Don't look at it, Cassie." My grandmother tried to push me away, but I resisted and strained my neck.

"M-M-Merry C-C-Christmas from C-C-Cassie."

Still in my socks, I ran to the front door and threw it open. I walked the couple of steps to the elevator where I smashed the down button. It couldn't open fast enough. Within a minute I was on ground level. I wanted to see the whole thing. I walked to the front of the apartment, which faced the street. Looking up, I saw a caricature of myself, my hair sticking out every which way, with a dialogue balloon next to me. It was a cartoon character of me stuttering for all the world to see. I let out a shriek.

"If that Noah and his friend Sam did this, I'll smack them all the way to Chicago." Mom waved her cereal spoon around making her point. My mother could be so dramatic, but it made me feel good. "Who is this brat, anyway?"

"Now we don't know he did it, or his friend," said Oma.

"I know it's him." I had no doubt. *Who else was so mean?*

"We'd best all calm down," said Opa, scooting his walker closer to me. "Let's not start accusing people until we know."

"But I heard him and his friend."

Mom stood, went to the kitchen for another cup of coffee, and sat down again. I watched the steam curl upwards towards the ceiling. "I have a mind to pack up everything and move back to Fayetteville."

"Let me remind you, you have a daughter to support and a job. Or I hope you have a job," said Oma.

"Ralph gave me a leave of absence, so my job isn't a problem. Anyway, no one is going to treat my girl this way. We're going to get to the bottom of this."

I suddenly had new respect for Mom. It was good to have her on your side when she was in a good mood. She'd fight for you.

Five minutes later, she came out of the bedroom, fully dressed with makeup on and her favorite earrings, the ones with three hoops that linked together like a chain. Mom never went anywhere without her earrings and bangle bracelets. She said it gave her style. Style or whatever, she had armed herself for battle. "I'm taking you to school. Get your boots on."

"You'll have to wait for Mr. Van Ark." Mrs. Groningen, the school administrative assistant, eyed my mother's arms full of bangle bracelets that clanked every time she moved. I swear Mom tried to annoy Mrs. Groningen with the clatter. Personally, I hoped it gave her courage. I needed a little myself. I turned and whispered in Mom's ear, "It's okay, let's forget about this whole thing."

Mom must have not heard me because she jumped up, jewelry clanking like a dozen wind chimes in a summer breeze. "Hello, Howard." She stretched out her hand to greet the principal. She must have known him when she grew up here to know his first name.

"Hello, Jillian. See you're a free woman now."

My mom waved her hand in the air like she had made it all go away. "All a big misunderstanding. Got it all cleared up. But that's not why I'm here."

"Speak." Mr. Van Ark ran his hand through what was left of his short black hair. He was always short on words.

"Can we use that conference room?" Mom pointed to a room adjoining the main office.

We found seats around the table. Mr. Van Ark closed the door, sat down, and cleared his throat. He blinked a lot. Mom could make people nervous when she had a mind to.

She placed her large red purse on the surface before lowering her gaze at Mr. Van Ark. "We've had our differences in the past, but this is about my daughter. Someone from school pranked her. We woke up to a nasty banner hanging from our balcony with a cartoon picture of Cassie wishing everyone a Merry Christmas."

"That doesn't sound too bad."

"They had Cassie stuttering in the cartoon."

"That is bad."

"Ya think? I don't want my daughter mocked."

"Of course not." Mr. Van Ark pulled a tissue from a box on the table, wrapped it around his big red nose, and blew. It sounded like he was honking a car horn. "I'm sure we can get to the bottom of this if we all calm down."

"Well, I hope you do. My daughter doesn't deserve to be treated like this."

"I couldn't agree more." He turned to me and smiled. "Is there someone who is angry with you? Some kid who wanted to embarrass you?"

"Uh, well, maybe."

"Go ahead and tell me their name."

"Do I have to?"

"We can't let this go. It's unacceptable for our students to mock anyone with a disability."

I took a deep breath, feeling like a snitch.

"Well, tell him," said Mom.

"Noah in my class."

Mr. Van Ark wrote down his name on a pad of paper. "I will be calling Noah in after I talk to you two to see if he knows anything about this inappropriate incident." He turned to Mom. "You know he's Nate and Tami Huizenga's kid."

"Tami's just next door to us." She picked up her purse. "I need to get to work." She kissed me on my forehead. "See you tonight."

# —Chapter Twenty-Three—

## Bell Ringing is Hard

"Are you sure you want to go out this afternoon?" Oma was frying mettwurst in an old cast-iron pan on the stove, along with some chopped red cabbage. The smell of the savory sausages mixed with her spicy applesauce cake baking in the oven filled me with hesitation. I had to choose between sitting in her cozy yellow kitchen and going downstairs in the freezing cold to ring my bell again. It was harder still because if I stayed, she'd give me a sliver of the burnt sugar-frosted cake when it cooled, even if it was only ten minutes to supper. She was like that. "Can't miss a chance at warm applesauce cake. Life's too short," she'd say and shush me, so Opa wouldn't find out and protest I was ruining my appetite for dinner. He was stricter like that. But only that way. Otherwise he was up for anything fun. Oma was strict but not with offering treats that ruined supper for me. I think it made her feel a little naughty.

"It's my last night, and I still need to collect more money."

"Well, you be careful. Remember, it gets dark at 5:00."

"It's only 3:30."

"I know, and I will keep peeking over the balcony. And of course Mrs. H. always knows what is going on in front of her store. I'll give her a ring just in case." She tsk-tsked a little with her tongue, and I knew that meant she had caught on to Mrs. H's nosiness.

I left the savory smells and warmth of the apartment and headed down the stairs to pull my kettle out of the outside closet in the alley. We stored it in the closet on days the Salvation Army guy couldn't come pick it up. I shivered as an icy wind attacked. Once set up, I slid my hand into my coat pocket to rub a copper lighthouse nickel for good luck. I figured it might help. Poppi had given it to me last Christmas. "It's to remind you to stand tall and shine wherever you go. Like a lighthouse." As the pale winter sun tried to punch through the clouds, I pulled the bell out of the other pocket and started ringing. It was kind of lonely. Marie Louise said her brother would drop her off, but I guess he couldn't.

My bell clanked, and even *it* sounded tired. This bell ringing was a lot of work. But I couldn't be selfish. I had to think of all those families I could help, even if I only had $45.22 total. I was hoping for fifty big ones. Fifty had a nice sound to it. Half a hundred.

Mrs. H. opened her store's door, poked her head out, and waved. "Just checking on you, dearie." She seemed to be a lot nicer lately. Maybe she knew I saved her boy from a pencil puncture.

A couple of middle school boys raced by, followed by their father, who looked irritated. Looked like they were heading toward Styles for the Family Hair Salon. No money there.

A very tall girl with long black hair down her back and wearing a Hope College sweatshirt stopped a minute. "You out here all alone?"

"N-n-no, n-n-not really."

"Looks like it." She frowned but dropped a ten-dollar bill into the kettle.

"Th-th-thanks."

"You'll get over it. The stuttering, I mean."

I didn't know what to say, so I nodded.

"I outgrew it." She waved and walked down the sidewalk and into the coffee shop two doors down where a guy met her at the door and gave her a hug. He was pretty cute. Maybe there's hope for me.

# —Chapter Twenty-Four—

## Dare to Sing

"Hey, Cas." I heard a familiar voice behind me. She DID come! I jumped up and down when I saw Marie Louise even if it had only been an hour since school let out. "Someone just gave me ten dollars."

"Really?"

"Really what?" I knew that voice from somewhere. Oh yeah, Noah.

"What are you doing here?" My excitement at seeing my best friend slid under a cloud of irritation.

"Came to see my mom, you know, Mrs. H., at the shop. Helping her today, but I'll be out later." He swung open the black lacquered door and popped inside.

"What's wrong with him?"

"That's not normal."

"It's some kind of trick, I bet. He's trying to mess up my last day."

"Don't worry. I have my mom's cell phone, and if there's any trouble, my brother Damion will be here in a flash." She waved the phone in front of me. We stood for a minute or two, watching some of the early evening shoppers bustle by.

"Brought my special coin. Want to see it?"

Marie Louise smiled, and I handed it to her. But somehow it slipped out of her hand. I watched it roll onto the sidewalk, and into a storm sewer. *Clink.*

"Oh no! I'm sorry," she said.

What could I say? I loved my coin. But I loved my friend more.

"It's okay. Maybe we can get those public works guys to open it next spring, and we can crawl down and find it."

"Yeah. Good idea. You have a bunch of friends over there. I still feel real bad."

I leaned over and gave her a big hug. "You're the best friend I've ever had. Who cares about a stupid coin?" I really did care, but I didn't want to tell her that.

We stood for a few more minutes with no one stopping when Marie Louise suggested we sing some Christmas carols.

"Don't you remember, we can't sing them?"

"Miss Hathaway isn't here. I dare you."

"Don't do d-dares," I said

"Chicken."

I knew I was. I also didn't want anyone to hear me sing. But her calling me chicken made me mad. I *was* brave. I moved to a new school, didn't I? And I rescued stupid Noah when he got stuck in the storm drain. That's pretty courageous.

"Well, maybe," I said as I yanked my hat lower over my ears.

"You start, because you're the official bell ringer."

*Dang, how does she talk me into these things?* "Well, okay. Maybe I'll sing 'Away in a Manger.'" I opened my mouth, but nothing came out except a little bitty squeak.

"You can do better," said Marie Louise, putting her hands on her hips for emphasis.

I tried again. "A-a-away in the mmmmmmmm." I clenched my hands together. "I can't do this."

"Yes, you can, I've heard you sing in choir. You have an awesome voice."

"You're just saying that."

"Try again."

I expanded my rib cage like my choir teacher taught us in Fayetteville. "Away in a manger, no crib for his bed."

"Keep going."

"The little Lord Jesus laid down his sweet head."

"Louder!"

"THE STARS IN THE SKY LOOKED DOWN WHERE HE LAY, THE LITTLE LORD JESUS ASLEEP IN THE HAY."

I watched as a kindly old man walked by and gave me a thumbs-up. How embarrassing, someone heard me.

"Okay, sing the next verse, and I'll ring the bell."

Mrs. H. poked her head out the door. "Love the carols, Cassie." I think that was a Christmas miracle for her to say that, but not exactly a golden moment. Still, it was nice for her to say something.

Marie Louise rang the bell, and I sang the second verse. It wasn't so hard once I started. The lump in my throat even disappeared. "The cattle are mowing ..."

I felt a sharp jab in my side.

"Not mowing, lowing," Marie Louise said.

"What's lowing?"

"I don't know, probably laying low. Just sing it."

"The cattle are lowing, the baby awakes, but little Lord Jesus no crying he makes. I love thee, Lord Jesus—"

"Amen to that," said Marie Louise.

"I love thee, Lord Jesus, look down from the sky and stay by my side until morning is nigh." I turned to Marie Louise. "What's nigh?"

"Heck if I know. Ask Miss Hathaway. Keep singing."

"Be near me, Lord Jesus, I ask you to stay, close by me forever and love me I pray …"

# —Chapter Twenty-Five—

## The Snitch

I stopped in the middle of the verse as I watched a small figure walking toward me. Jessimyn. I knew it was her because she had the largest red-and-white-striped toboggan hat in school, to remind everyone she was going to play the head elf in the school holiday play. Marie Louise and I figured she got the part because her dad was the school superintendent. She always had an in for those starring roles, at least that's what Marie Louise said.

"Mom's shopping at Pursley's jewelry store and said I could put in some money." She fished around in her little coin purse, the one with a big yellow cross on it, and dropped a couple of dimes and nickels.

"Thanks," I said.

"Want to sing with us?' said Marie Louise. She elbowed me for the second time that day.

"Away in a manger," I sang again.

"No crib for his bed," finished Marie Louise.

Jessimyn's mouth dropped open. "You're not supposed to sing Christmas carols. Don't you know the rules?"

"And who's going to tell?"

"You're such a Grinch, Jessimyn." I got brave and took a step toward her. She backed up.

"You're in trouble, Cassie. You probably will get a big fat zero on the project."

Marie Louise shoved Jessimyn, who fell on her butt on the sidewalk.

"Wait 'til I …"

"Wait 'til what?" a voice behind me boomed. I froze. Noah again. Oh no, two of my most not-favorite people at the same time. How unlucky can a person be? He'd probably walk back with Jessimyn to Pursley's and report me to her mom.

"I'm not quitting," I said.

Jessimyn narrowed her eyes. "I just recorded this on my phone. Wait 'til I show this to Ms. Hathaway. You're going to flunk the project. And the school board will probably come talk to your mother and kick you out of school. You heard her talk about no religious stuff."

"Since when are you Miss Hathaway's spy?"

"She likes me a lot. I let her know what is going on and what's going on is YOU'RE NOT FOLLOWING THE RULES, CASSIE."

I clenched my jaw. I didn't want any more trouble. Still, I thought about my dad's words about Joshua the spy in the Old Testament. I could almost hear his voice saying, "Be strong and courageous." My father was the bravest person I knew. Why couldn't I be brave and sing? I shuddered. The big mouth of Maple Leaf Elementary could make my life miserable. But my father's words shouted louder. The longer I waited the louder they grew.

"Away in a manger, no crib for his bed."

"That's it. You have an epic voice." Noah opened his mouth and joined in. I turned to him, amazed at his strong, clear sound. He should be in choir.

"Jessimyn, I'm finished," Mrs. Snyder hollered from across the street.

"Sing louder," said Marie Louise, clacking the bell as hard as she could. I wondered if she was trying to use it to ward off Mrs. Snyder.

Mrs. Snyder crossed the street, and my stomach felt like two of Oma's knitting needles were poking my insides. *Here goes, I'll probably get kicked out of school.*

Jessimyn rushed to her mother and started to say something. Her mother turned and shushed her. "Oh, how sweet," said Mrs. Snyder. "Here, Jessimyn, here's a five. Drop it in the kettle."

Jessimyn looked at her mother with a puzzled look. "But, Mom, they're …"

"Yes, I think we should put them all in jail, Jessimyn," she answered and jerked her daughter's arm. "When are you going to keep your nose out of other people's business?" She dropped Jessimyn's arm and pulled her handbag back on her shoulder before looking up. She caught a look at my mother, who had crept up next to my kettle. "Well, if it isn't a blast from the past. Hello, Jillian." She walked over to Mom, her boots scuffing against the sidewalk, and enveloped her in a hug. "I have been meaning to call you. So good to see you again. I understand you are on the road a lot."

"Yes," said my mother. She seemed to be pretty happy to see Mrs. Snyder. "I do travel a lot but am home for a few days."

"We'll have to do coffee. What are your evenings like?"

"I'm free tomorrow." Did my mother's face light up? She hadn't smiled much since the big "Incident" that landed her in the county jail.

"Your daughter is adorable. The spitting image of you as a kid."

*Wow, that's a good sign.* My mother was beautiful, and I hoped I had those genes.

"Give me your phone number, and I'll give you a ring," said Mom. I was so happy she had a friend again. Mom pulled out her phone and added Mrs. Snyder to her contacts. "Done."

They chatted a few moments about the upcoming class reunion and their adventures cheerleading in high school when Mrs. Snyder said, "Whatever happened to the other one?"

My mother dropped her purse as her body thudded against the lamppost. She started to breathe hard. I wondered if someone should call 911. Was she going to faint?

The bell ringing stopped. The song ended, and I eyed my mother. "What other one?" It came out in a shriek. I wanted to put more words into the air, but I couldn't find them. Maybe *I* needed someone to call 911.

"It's a long story." I had a feeling my whole life was about to change.

# —Chapter Twenty-Six—

## *Mom's Story*

Me, Opa, and Oma sat lined up on the sofa at my grandparents' house. Oma had her hands crossed over her chest, Opa pinched the bridge of his nose above his glasses, and Mom paced the carpet in front of the coffee table. She must have walked the route fifteen times before she spoke.

"Cassie, I need to tell you a story."

"S-s-story? I don't want a story."

"Zip your mouth and listen." She stopped and looked at me. "I should have told you before but there was never the right time." She wrung her hands together and continued. "You know I grew up here. Well, I went away to college at Central and studied business. I always knew I wanted to go into sales and marketing, so when I finished, I was offered a job at Herman Miller. It was my perfect job, and I worked a lot of long hours. I also fell in love with my boss's son, Kyle."

"There was someone before Dad?"

"Let me finish." She started her pacing again, my eyes glued on her plaid skirt that moved back and forth with her, like a flag. "We eloped and were secretly married because his father didn't approve of me. Thought I was too flighty. So we fought a lot until he left. The next week I found out I was two months pregnant. I was very worried about how I was going to support a child. By then Kyle had moved out of town, and I couldn't get in touch with him. He wouldn't return my phone calls."

"So Poppi isn't my biological dad?" If a horse had kicked me in the stomach, it wouldn't have felt worse.

Mom walked over to me and took my hand, pressing it tightly. "No, he isn't, honey. Your biological father and I were both very young. So anyway, I moved in with Mom and Dad for a while, but I knew that wouldn't work either. I felt like I was a burden."

"You're not a burden," said Opa.

I didn't say anything. I was still thinking about what Mom said. *Poppi isn't my real father.*

"Well, I knew I would be when I saw the ultrasound. Two little figures. Two heads, two bodies, four hands, four feet. I drove home from the doctor and locked myself in my room for a day. I didn't tell Oma and Opa for a while."

"Kind of hard to hide twins with a growing belly," said Oma.

"Yes. So I kept trying to contact Kyle. Finally, he served me divorce papers, two days before I was to give birth. I remember lying in that hospital feeling like all the world had abandoned me. How could I possibly support two children? Still, I really wanted to be a mother. The nurse rolled both of you in, and I looked at you two with wonder and fear. Then I closed my eyes and prayed, "God, which one?" I opened my eyes, and you were waving your tiny hand at me. I knew that was a sign. I talked to the hospital staff and explained what I was thinking. They put me in touch with Bethany Adoption Services. Your birth father signed off on any responsibility. In a couple of days I left the hospital with the most beautiful baby girl in the world."

"But the other baby?"

"The other twin was adopted by an out-of-town couple." Mom stopped her pacing and kneeled down in front of me, her nose twitching like it always does when she's nervous.

I bit my lip, holding back tears, with so many emotions swirling in my head. Then I thought about how I had a twin. A sibling. "Mom, why didn't you tell me sooner? And who is Dad?"

She took both my hands in hers. "I was going to when you were older." She dropped my hands and dabbed her eyes with a tissue before starting to pace again. "Let me finish my story. When you were two years old, I was able to transfer my job south, so we moved to Fayetteville. Do you remember?"

"No."

"We had moved to a military town. I went on a double date with one of my co-workers who set me up and met your dad. His kind personality, stability, and charm swept me off my feet, as they say. And, of course, he loved you. The second time we went out, he *insisted* I bring my daughter."

"I remember you calling me, Jillian, and telling me how much he was taken with Cassie," said Oma, putting her arm around me. The warmth of her arm around my shoulder helped me listen better to the big news.

"I told him about my history, and it didn't seem to bother him. He loved me for who I was now. And yes, he knew about the other twin."

Frustration bubbled inside of me. I thought I would explode with this new view of life. I was surprised, scared, and not just a little mad at Mom. "How could you … how could you give away…" I swallowed and took a deep breath. The loss in my mother's eyes was enough to stop me from asking what had to have been a hard choice. "So, where's my twin? Do you know where she is? Do I get to meet her?"

"If you like." My mother pulled her phone out of her jeans pocket and dialed. "Yes, is it okay with your mother? Okay, then come up by the side elevator, get off, and ring the front door. We're waiting for you."

# —Chapter Twenty-Seven—

## A Golden Moment

Her phone call sucked all noise from the room as we waited in painful silence. Then the elevator's motor rumbled as it moved up the side of the apartment before jerking to a stop. I heard the soft padding of snow boots walking to the front door. The doorbell rang, and we all looked at each other. Mom stood and went around the corner, out of view, to open it.

Mom entered the room, turned, and beckoned at a shadow still standing in the hallway. I strained my eyes but couldn't see much until …

"Noah?"

I hoped the way I said it didn't express the horror I felt, but when I looked at his face, I knew he caught it. He looked down at his feet. I didn't know what to do.

He looked up at Mom and then at me. "Hi, Sis." And out of nowhere his mouth started to turn up, little by little, until it turned into a full-sized grin. And, it was a real grin, not a smirk, or a mock, but a genuine, bona fide, real smile. He put out his hand.

*Now what the heck was I supposed to do? I guess shake it.* I reached out my hand and touched his and withdrew it as soon as I could. After all, I wasn't used to having a brother, one that was my enemy. Never read a book about it, never saw a show. This was new territory.

"Noah was adopted as a baby. He just found out, too, so he's a bit surprised," said Opa. "And so were we. Our own grandson living right here in town.

According to the Huizengas, they moved here five years ago from Ludington." He pulled himself off the couch and gripped the handles of his walker, edging it towards Noah. Oma surpassed him as she ran to hug Noah.

I felt real funny seeing that. After all, Oma and Opa were *my* own grandparents. Was I supposed to share them now? Why him? Why not a nice twin?

But then I thought about how he sang with me. *Maybe he isn't so bad after all.*

Mom and Opa and Oma gathered together in one big hug with Noah in the middle. I watched. This was the strangest thing I'd ever been through. Still, my grandparents' faces shone with joy as Opa rumpled up Noah's hair and Oma took both of his hands so she could stare at him.

"He looks a lot like Uncle Gerald," Oma said. "It's those hazel eyes."

"Yes, and I'll bet you're athletic," said Opa.

"His mother said he's a basketball whiz. Practices every day," said Mom. She pinched his cheek. "This is a dream come true."

Through all of the commotion and displays of affection, Noah said nothing. I wondered what was going on in his head. Finally, he slipped out of the group hug and walked up to me. "So, what do you think, Sis?"

"It feels f-f-funny to hear someone call me that, especially the guy I hated the most at school."

"Cassie!" said my mother.

"It's true," said Noah. "I was a jerk."

She took both my hands. "I know this is a shock for you. I should have told you sooner, but it was never the right time. I only found out when Mrs. Huizenga called me to apologize about Noah putting that banner up." She dropped one of my hands and took one of Noah's. "She told me that when she got sick, she searched for me. Kept the information just … in case. I finally met him the day she called me."

I only walked him to the elevator 'cause Mom said it was the right thing to do. Polite. He mashed the button to go down, but it didn't respond. He pushed it again. Nothing.

He turned to me. "Guess I need to tell you sorry."

"Th-th-that would be okay."

"Well, I found out about you a couple of months ago. My mom first said I should wait until we were older. She admitted to being afraid to lose me, but I told her no matter what, she's my mom, the one who raised me. It really bugged me that I had a sister and that your mom chose you instead of me. That's why I was so mean to you. But when you helped me like a sister would, like a twin, by saving my forehead from a pencil …"

"And getting help so you could get out of the manhole."

"Anyway, I finally realized I *wanted* to have a sister, and better still, a twin." He pushed the elevator button again, and the steel door jerked and finally opened. "By the way, even though we're fraternal twins, we share one thing."

"What?"

He pointed to the cleft in his chin. "That's how I believed my mom when she told me about you and your mom … our mom. We both have butt chins."

"It's so weird to think we're twins. Same birthday, same birth mom." I giggled. "Weird is okay. I like weird."

"That's because you are."

He slugged my arm before stepping into the elevator and then waved. "See you at school."

The door closed, and I rubbed my arm on the spot where he hit me.

Mom came out through the sliding glass door. "Are you mad at me?"

"No, Mom. I'm glad we moved here."

"Ah, my sweet girl." She stroked my hair. "Sorry I've put you through so much."

"It's okay. I got my wish. I have a brother."

We stood on the balcony for a moment as feathery snowflakes sashayed their way onto my face. No shining sun, no warmth, only the icy air that makes for a Michigan winter.  I rubbed my arm once more to remember I had a brother. It kinda felt good. Sorta brotherly, if that's a word. Guess there are still more miracles around.

Dear Poppi,

Things improved a lot in my life since that afternoon I found out I had a brother. Noah says "Hi" to me and the kids in our school think it's cool we're twins, so that makes *me* cool by association. The mouth of the school, Jessimyn, never told about our singing Christmas carols and Miss Hathaway gave me a 100 percent on my project. I'm getting used to winter and even tried cross-country skiing with Marie Louise and her family. Mom doesn't have travel overnight anymore. And best of all, you're coming home in three weeks when you get transferred to Grand Rapids, so we can drive to visit you.

I never really understood when you talked about Golden Moments, but I wanted to let you know. Poppi, I get it.

I can't wait to see you.

Love,
Cassie

Made in the USA
Monee, IL
06 December 2020

51219117R00111